The Race to Rule
Ireland and Europe
1570–1700

Audrey M Hodge

Colourpoint
Educational

First Edition
Seventh Impression

ISBN: 978 1898392 49 1

Printed by: W&G Baird Ltd

Cover illustration by Henry Ford, from *A History of England* by CRL Fletcher and Rudyard Kipling

COLOURPOINT BOOKS

Colourpoint House
Jubilee Business Park
21 Jubilee Road
Newtownards
Co Down
BT23 4YH

Tel: (028) 9182 6339
Fax: (028) 9182 1900
E-mail: info@colourpoint.co.uk
Web site: www.colourpoint.co.uk

The author

Audrey Hodge is a Senior Teacher at Omagh Academy, Co Tyrone. She obtained her MA in Modern and Contemporary History at the University of Ulster. She is co-author of *Union to Partition* (Colourpoint 1995) and of *The Race to Rule's* fore-runner, *Britain, Ireland and Europe from 1570–1745*. She has also written *Gallows and Turnkeys* which is a short history of Omagh Gaol, and *A Congregation in the Omey* (1997) which is a history of First Omagh Presbyterian Church.

Acknowledgements

Hulton Getty Picture Library 7, 8, 9, 13, 18, 22, 24, 25, 37, 39, 51, 53, 55, 58, 60, 66, 67.
Mary Evans Picture Library 11, 19.
National Galleries of Scotland 15, 17, 19, 52 (top), 69.
Audrey Hodge 23.
John Brogan 29, 33, 56A, 57C, 72.
Ulster Museum 30, 31.
Ulster History Park 40, 44.
N Johnston 45, 76.
© Crown copyright. Reproduced with the permission of the Controller of HMSO 45.
National Gallery of Ireland 70
Dr W Maguire 74

The publisher will be glad to be notified of any credits inadvertently omitted.

Contents

Introduction

The period from the first Tudor monarch, Henry VII in 1485, until the arrival of a Hanoverian monarch, George I in 1714, witnessed great changes in Britain.

Many famous events took place also at this time. Henry VIII had six wives, Mary Queen of Scots was beheaded, the Spanish Armada was defeated, and the English Civil War and the famous battles at the Boyne and Aughrim took place.

This is therefore a period full of romance, intrigue and adventure.

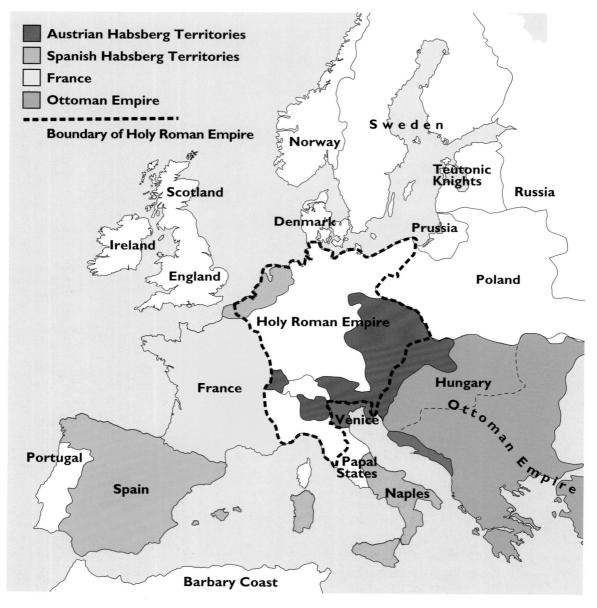

Europe in 1570

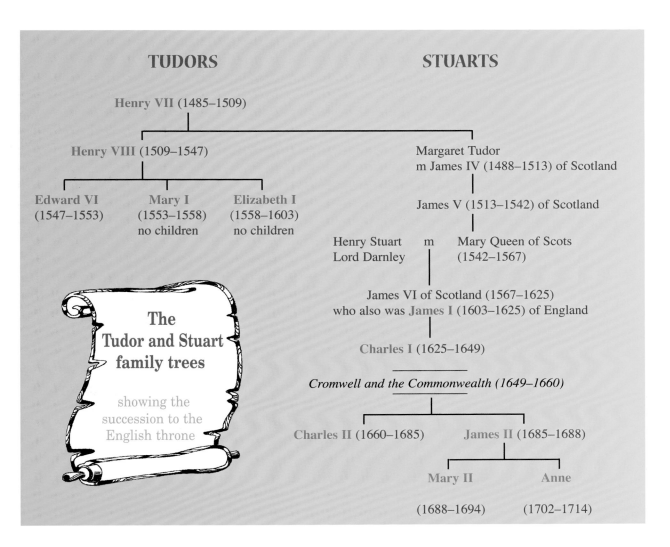

TUDORS

Henry VII (1485–1509)

Henry VIII (1509–1547)

Edward VI
(1547–1553)

Mary I
(1553–1558)
no children

Elizabeth I
(1558–1603)
no children

STUARTS

Margaret Tudor
m James IV (1488–1513) of Scotland

James V (1513–1542) of Scotland

Henry Stuart   m   Mary Queen of Scots
Lord Darnley   (1542–1567)

James VI of Scotland (1567–1625)
who also was James I (1603–1625) of England

Charles I (1625–1649)

Cromwell and the Commonwealth (1649–1660)

Charles II (1660–1685)   James II (1685–1688)

Mary II   Anne

(1688–1694)   (1702–1714)

The Tudor and Stuart family trees

showing the succession to the English throne

Henry VIII and his six wives

Catherine of Aragon	—	*Divorced*
Anne Boleyn	—	*Beheaded*
Jane Seymour	—	*Died*
Anne of Cleves	—	*Divorced*
Catherine Howard	—	*Beheaded*
Catherine Parr	—	*Survived*

5

1.1 Elizabethan England

Henry VIII's second daughter, **Elizabeth**, became Queen in **1558**, after the death of her elder sister **Mary Tudor**.

At this time, England was facing a major religious crisis. During the preceding 30 years, many people had died because of their religion. Some had died during the reign of Edward VI because they were Roman Catholics and many had died during Mary's reign because they were Protestants.

In 1558 Elizabeth was hoping to find a middle way in religion but such a compromise did not please many. In 1570 the Pope **excommunicated** Elizabeth and, from then on, she can be regarded as a Protestant.

Religious problems

Those who refused to accept this new Elizabethan church were called **recusants**. Many of them had to pay heavy fines for non attendance at the Protestant church; others even lost their lands. Many Roman Catholic missionary priests came to England and were persecuted for trying to spread their message there. The Queen's Principal Secretary, Sir Francis Walsingham, led the campaign against these priests.

The persecution did not discourage many and in the homes of wealthy recusants **priest hides** were built (Source C).

C

A priest's hide

A

Walsingham shows in his behaviour unmistakable marks of brutality and fanaticism. Blinded by religious passion he believed every Catholic priest was dangerous to the state and he conducted their examination in person.

Quoted in: *Elizabeth in Danger*, SM Harrison, Macmillan 1990

B

Walsingham was, on the whole, opposed to the execution of priests 'saving a few for example's sake'. Taken as a whole his policy was a policy of mercy. The result of his advice eased considerably the fate of the missionary priest.

Quoted in: *Elizabeth in Danger*, SM Harrison, Macmillan 1990

excommunicate – to cut off a person from the church
recusant – a person who refused to accept a new religion
wainscot – wooden panelling around the walls of a room

D

Concealed in a cupboard behind the wainscot of a room for a few days ... at the end of that time ... was released from the hiding hole half dead.

Father Gerard, a missionary priest describing his personal experience

E

The Globe Theatre, 1612

The Elizabethan theatre

A more pleasant side to life in Elizabethan England was the development of the theatre and the associated plays of William Shakespeare. Many playhouses were built in London and around the country, the most famous of which was the **Globe Theatre** in **Stratford-on-Avon** (Source E). A flag on top of the theatre indicated that a play would be performed that day. The early plays were performed in inn yards and this was reflected in the shape of these new theatres. Women were not permitted to act, so young boys always played the female parts.

The early plays performed in inn yards often caused problems of crowd control. The audience were tightly packed and drink was widely available. On occasions, there was so much trouble at these plays that the London authorities banned them.

Some reasons for banning inn yard plays:
◆ Disorderly conduct, especially by the young
◆ Fights have broken out
◆ Plays encourage immorality
◆ Plays keep people from going to church
◆ They are a waste of money
◆ Pickpockets are encouraged to operate during plays
◆ The collapse of temporary stages leads to injuries
◆ Plague spreads among the closely packed audiences

Because they were limited in scenery and lighting, words describing these were usually included in the plays (Source G).

G

But look how the morn in russet mantle clad walks o'er the dew of yon high eastern hill.

William Shakespeare, *Hamlet*

F

Of the means or instruments of torture employed in the Tower there are seven different kinds. The first is the Pit, a subterraneous cave twenty feet deep and entirely without light. The second is a cell or dungeon so small as to be incapable of admitting a person in erect posture ... The third is the rack, on which ... the limbs of the sufferer are drawn in opposite directions. The fourth is called the 'scavenger's daughter'. It consists of an iron ring which brings the head, feet and hands together until they form a circle. The fifth is the iron gauntlet, which encloses the hand with the most excruciating pain. The sixth consists of chains or manacles attached to the arms, and the seventh of fetters by which the feet are confined.

Edward Rishton, a prisoner in the Tower of London

Activity

Find some other Shakespearean plays and look for descriptions of scenery and lighting.

Questions

1 Identify those words or phrases in Sources A and B which show how the writers differ about Walsingham's treatment of these priests.

2 Explain why such contradictory views exist.

3 Using Source F rank order the seven different kinds of torture used in the Tower.

4 Look at Source G. Which time of day is portrayed in this section? What sort of terrain is being portrayed?

1.2 Reformation and Luther

Until the early sixteenth century the Roman Catholic church was the church to which Christian people in western Europe belonged. However, many were beginning to become very dissatisfied with the church and its leaders. Some popes had not been good examples such as Rodrigo Borgia who was elected Pope Alexander VI in the 1490s (Source A).

Even the bishops were often poor examples of good behaviour. Jean de Lorainne, a French nobleman, became a bishop at the age of three. Later he was made bishop over nine more dioceses and abbot of nine monasteries. King Ferdinand of Aragon got appointments in the church for his illegitimate children, and Pope Sextus IV made his nephews cardinals.

It is not surprising then that some ordinary priests and monks were not good examples either.

Many ordinary people were very ignorant about their religion. They did not understand much of their church services which were in Latin. Beliefs in witchcraft and superstitions were widespread.

People who wished to change or reform the church were known as Reformers. Some of these were **Sir Thomas More**, **Erasmus** of Rotterdam, **Girolamo Savonarola** and, the best known, **Martin Luther**.

A painting of Martin Luther by the artist Noel Paton

A

Borgia openly bribed many of the cardinals, some with money, others with promises of profitable jobs, of which he had many at that time in his power.

Written in 1490s referring to Borgia's election

B

A monk there was, one of the finest sort who rode the country; hunting was his sport ... Hunting a hare or riding at a fence was all his fun, he spared for no expense.

From the *Canterbury Tales* by Geoffrey Chaucer

C

They lack all education. They understand nothing at all of what they sing. The holy scriptures are never seen in their hands. They never discuss or preach and they take no account of training in morals.

A German monk writing about other monks in 1493

D

I would have become a martyr through fasting, prayer, reading and other good works had I remained a monk much longer.

Martin Luther

E

The next day Dr Luther warned us that it was easy to burn the Pope's letter and books. But we needed to end completely the rule of the Pope. Dr Luther said it would be better to live lonely in a desert than under the laws of the Pope.

A student who witnessed the burning of the Pope's letter

Martin Luther was born in Eisleben, in Saxony, in **1483**. When he was 17 years old he went to the University of Erfurt and during his time there he decided to become a monk. He lived a very strict life, but was not really happy.

Luther became particularly angry over the church's sale of **indulgences** to help raise money to rebuild St Peter's Cathedral in Rome.

Indulgence meant you could help yourself to spend less time in Purgatory suffering for your sins if you did good works such as giving money to the church.

In **1517** Luther nailed to the door of Wittenberg church a list of 95 points which he wished to have discussed. These were known as the **95 Theses**. His outspoken ideas made many church leaders, including the Pope, very angry. The Pope wrote to Luther demanding that he retract these criticisms or be excommunicated. In 1520 Luther burned the Pope's letter.

Luther read the Bible carefully and he also wrote several pamphlets which were read eagerly by many. In fact Luther became a sort of hero to many Germans.

Martin Luther burning the Pope's letter

Luther was summoned to a special court called a **Diet** at **Worms** in **1521**.

The Emperor Charles V ordered Luther to go home and stop his preaching. Luther began to translate the New Testament into German as well as writing some hymns. For almost a year, he stayed away from any open controversy.

His followers were known as **Lutherans** or **Protestants** because they protested against the teaching of the Roman Catholic Church.

Luther married a former nun, Catherine von Bora, in 1525 and they had 6 children (3 sons and 3 daughters). He died in 1546.

This great change, or **Reformation**, spread from Germany across Europe and eventually all over the world.

Activity

Construct a time line for the life of Luther, using these dates: 1483, 1500, 1517, 1520, 1521, 1525, 1546.

Questions

What criticisms could be levelled at the church? Do you think they were justified?
Explain your answer.

1.3 Rivalries in Europe

Activity

1 Discuss with a partner, or in small groups, the factors which make a country powerful. Put them in order and discuss your reasons.

2 Compare your group's answers with the rest of the class. Try to come to class agreement on their order of importance.

3 Using these criteria, place Spain, France and the Holy Roman Empire in order of importance.

Let us consider what makes one country more powerful than another. Three factors are particularly important:

(a) **Geographical size.** Compare the Holy Roman Empire with Venice.

(b) **Population.** A larger population allowed a ruler to have a bigger army which gave him more power.

(c) **Wealth.** Trade made several countries very rich. This could compensate for being small in size or population. For this reason England and Venice, although small, could afford to have powerful navies. Spain and Portugal had overseas empires in America.

In eastern Europe the most powerful states were Sweden, Poland, Russia and the Ottoman Empire. We are mainly concerned with western Europe in which three states were powerful in 1570.

Spain

Ruler: Philip II (1556–1598)

Religion: Catholic

Economy: Mainly agriculture. Immense wealth due to imported silver from central and southern America (The New World).

Armed Forces: Large navy and powerful army

Politics: Rival of France. Controlled Low Countries (Holland and Belgium).

France

Ruler: Charles IX (1560–1574)

Religion: Mainly Catholic, but some Protestants

Economy: Agriculture, trade and industry

Armed Forces: Good army and navy

Politics: Rival of Spain

Holy Roman Empire

Ruler: Maximilian II (1564–1576))

Religion: Catholic and Protestant

Economy: Agriculture, trade and industry

Armed Forces: Each state had its own army.

Politics: Maximilian was an Emperor ruling a loose federation (group) of independent states. The Empire had little real unity.

A

The massacre of St Bartholomew. This event took place on 24 August 1572

Dynastic wars

Each European state was ruled by a royal family or dynasty which handed on the crown from father to son. The most powerful family in Europe was the **Habsburg family** whose emperor was Charles V (1519–1556). He was also the Holy Roman Emperor. The main challenge to the power of the Habsburgs came from the **Valois** dynasty in France. There had been many wars involving other countries because of alliances and marriages. Mary Queen of Scots had married the French King. Henry VIII had married a Spanish princess. Philip II of Spain had married Mary Tudor and hoped to marry her sister, Elizabeth.

Civil wars are between two groups within a country. There were many of these in France often caused by religion. In 1572 French Protestants, known as **Huguenots**, were massacred in Paris and elsewhere on 24 August which was St Bartholomew's Day. Estimates of the numbers of deaths vary from 6,000 to 50,000 in just a few days.

Religious wars

The Reformation caused bitter divisions between Protestants and Catholics throughout Europe. In 1534 a priest called **Ignatius Loyola** formed the **Society of Jesus (Jesuits)** to reconvert people in Protestant countries. In other countries such as Spain and Italy, where there were few Protestants, a sort of religious court of law, called **The Inquisition**, was used to try to stamp out this 'new' religion of Protestantism. Terrible tortures were used, including the burning at the stake of people who would not conform.

Questions

1 Explain the meaning of the following terms: dynasty; Habsburgs; Reformation; Jesuit; Inquisition; Huguenot.

2 What does Source A tell us about the massacre?

3 How useful are pictures such as Source A to a historian? Explain your answer.

1.4   Sailors and explorers

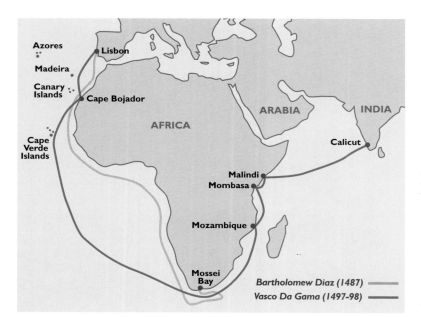

Left: The voyages of Bartholomew Diaz and Vasco De Gama

As European countries became more powerful, they sought new territories and also new routes to bring goods from these colonies to Europe.

In 1487 a Portuguese sailor called **Bartholomew Diaz** set sail from Lisbon and travelled south, going further than any other sailor had before. In early January 1488 a storm blew his ships off course and Diaz discovered that he had passed the southern tip of Africa, which he named 'Cape of Storms'. On his return to Portugal, the King renamed it 'Cape of Good Hope'.

Another Portuguese sailor, **Vasco Da Gama**, set sail from Lisbon in July 1497. It was his intention to sail past the Cape of Good Hope and reach India eventually. Once he had succeeded in doing this, other sailors found their way to the Spice Islands. All of this helped Portugal to become a great empire.

Christopher Columbus was a poor Italian sailor who wished to make a fortune but needed support for his proposed voyage westwards to find another route to the Spice Islands. The King of Portugal turned him down but he got support from the King and Queen of Spain.

Columbus had three ships for his voyage – the *Sancta Maria*, the *Nina*, and the *Pinta*. They left Spain in August 1492, sailing west across the Atlantic Ocean. In October they reached land which Columbus named San Salvador (The Holy Saviour). Today this is Watling Island in the Bahamas. Columbus thought he had arrived in India so he called the lands which he had found the 'West Indies'.

He went on to sail to other islands such as Cuba where they saw "men eating smoke". What do you think these men were really doing?

Columbus visited many of these islands but never found large quantities of spices or wealth. When he died in 1506 he did not realise that he had discovered a 'New World' of North and South America. Instead, he was very disappointed that neither he nor the King had gained great wealth from these voyages.

These voyages helped persuade people that the world may be round rather than flat, but no one had *proved* that the world was round. The first sailor to circumnavigate the world was another Portuguese, **Ferdinand Magellan**. King Charles V of Spain agreed to support him. He set sail in April 1519.

Magellan had five ships: the *Santiago, Victoria, Conception, Trinity* and *San Antonio*.

Magellan's ship was the *Trinity* which weighed 110 tonnes. The modern Stena Caledonia, which sails the Belfast–Stranraer route, weighs about 12,000 tonnes.

They took enough food for two years.
For example, on board the *Victoria* was:

2 tons dried biscuits	19lbs sugar
1 ton salted meat and fish	30lbs mustard
1/2 ton beans, lentils and peas	
4 crates marmalade	475lbs cheese
3 basket figs	30 barrels anchovies
8 barrels dried plums	82 casks wine
almonds & honey	50 bundles garlic

After an eventful journey with mutinies and the loss of four ships, the *Victoria* sailed into Seville in September 1522 with only 18 men on board, all of them sick. The Italian crewman, Pigafetta, kept a journal and he described the death of Magellan in the Philippines in April 1521 (Source C).

Magellan's voyage 1519–22 was the first journey around the world. The first Englishman to do so was **Sir Francis Drake** 1577–1580. You will learn about him in Unit 1.9.

Columbus encouraging his men on their voyage to the New World

B

The natives go as naked as when their mothers bore them. They are very well made ... their hair is short and coarse. I believe that they will easily become Christians because they seem to have no religion of their own ... I think they would make good servants because I noticed how quickly they understood what was said to them.

Columbus' description of West Indian natives

C

The Captain General was shot through the right arm with a poisoned arrow ... so many of (the natives) attacked the Captain General that they knock his helmet off twice ... He always stood firm like a good knight ...They charged at him again with bamboo spears and cutlasses until they had killed our mirror, our light, our comfort and our true guide.

Pigafetta, crewman on the *Victoria*

circumnavigate – to travel all the way around

Questions

1 **Suggest why Da Gama took so much with him for the 'King of Calicut'. What do you think his feelings about his voyage were?**

2 **Read Source B. Why did Columbus think these people would become a) Christians and b) good servants?**

3 **In what ways was food preserved on board ship?**

4 **Why was there so much mustard and garlic?**

5 **What evidence is there that Pigafetta thought highly of Magellan?**

1.5 Mary's early life

Mary Queen of Scots was born in Scotland in 1542, the daughter of the Scottish King James V and his Queen, a French princess, Mary of Guise. James was already near death, worn out by the intrigues of France, England and his own noblemen. He died when Mary was less than a week old. When he received the news of her birth he recalled how the throne had come to his family through Margery Bruce: "It came with a lass, and it will gang [go] with a lass." Then he laughed and fell back dead! Mary was Queen of Scotland, perhaps history's youngest Queen. She was to live for 45 years – a turbulent and troubled life of disastrous marriages, intrigues, murders, plots and eventually imprisonment and execution.

Mary's early life

Mary of Guise tried to rule Scotland as regent for her young daughter. She sent Mary to live in France at the age of six (1548) when she was betrothed to **Francis**, the four year old son of the French King Henry II. They were married ten years later in 1558. Shortly after, Henry II was killed in a tournament accident and Francis became King (1559). Mary was Queen of France. Her glory was shortlived, however, as her young husband was sickly and died in 1560. At the age of 18 Mary was a widow. Back in Scotland her mother had also died in 1560. No longer Queen of France, Mary decided to return to Scotland in 1561.

A

She had a marvellous way of talking – gentle and feminine, and with kindly majesty. Her speech was modest and reserved, and very graceful. When she spoke Scottish (which is a very barbarous, ill-sounding and rough language) she made it sound beautiful and pleasant – which no one else can.

Brantôme, a French writer writing about 1558

regent – someone in charge of a kingdom at times when the monarch is not able to rule

betrothed – engaged to be married

B

Francis, aged about 14

Activity

Construct a timeline of Mary's life from her birth in 1542 until her death in 1587. Using the information in this unit, fill it in until 1561.

Mary Queen of Scots, painted wearing mourning clothes after the death of her young husband Francis in 1560

D

D

To promote a woman to bear rule, superiority, dominion or empire over any realm, nation or city is repugnant to nature and contumely (insulting) to God. It is a thing most contrary to his revealed will and approved ordinance (decree). Finally, it is the subversion of good order, equity and justice.

Quoted from *The First Blast of the Trumpet Against the Monstrous Regiment of Women,* John Knox, 1558

The Reformation in Scotland

Inside Scotland things had been changing. The old alliance with France was no longer popular. England had become Protestant and in Scotland many of the noblemen had converted to Protestantism, including Mary's half-brother James Stewart. (Mary used the French version of her name – Stuart.) They now wanted Scotland to be allied to England, rather than Catholic France. The Reformation in England had been briefly halted during the reign of Mary I (1553–58), who was Roman Catholic. (This was Mary Tudor, not to be confused with Mary Queen of Scots.) But in 1558 the Protestant Elizabeth I (1558–1603) had become Queen of England. The Scottish nobles did not want a Catholic Queen, and Mary Queen of Scots was a practising Catholic. As soon as Mary arrived in Scotland there was opposition. The fiercest opposition came from **John Knox**, a fiery Protestant preacher, who was highly critical of Mary. He gave her strong advice on how she should dress and who she should marry. He obviously did not like women to be in a position of authority, as Source D shows.

1 What are the differences between the views of Brantôme and John Knox regarding Mary? (Sources A and D)

2 Explain why these two men may have viewed Mary differently.

Questions

1.6 Mary Queen of Scotland

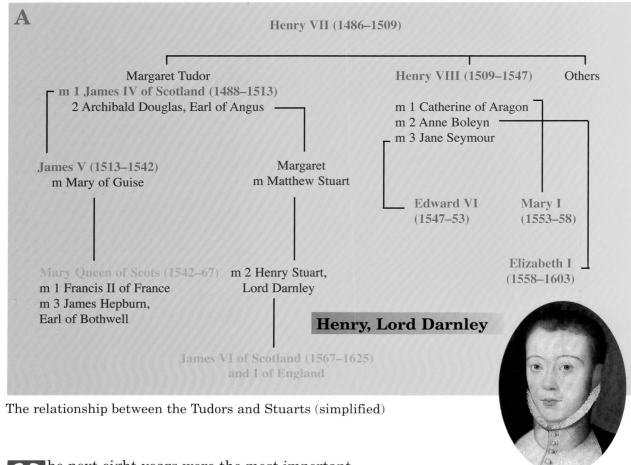

A

Henry VII (1486–1509)

Margaret Tudor
m 1 James IV of Scotland (1488–1513)
2 Archibald Douglas, Earl of Angus

Henry VIII (1509–1547)   Others

m 1 Catherine of Aragon
m 2 Anne Boleyn
m 3 Jane Seymour

James V (1513–1542)
m Mary of Guise

Margaret
m Matthew Stuart

Edward VI
(1547–53)

Mary I
(1553–58)

Elizabeth I
(1558–1603)

Mary Queen of Scots (1542–67)
m 1 Francis II of France
m 3 James Hepburn,
Earl of Bothwell

m 2 Henry Stuart,
Lord Darnley

Henry, Lord Darnley

James VI of Scotland (1567–1625)
and I of England

The relationship between the Tudors and Stuarts (simplified)

The next eight years were the most important in Mary's life. Scandal seemed to pursue her wherever she went. Mary did not persecute the Protestants, but she remained Catholic herself. In 1565 she married **Henry, Lord Darnley**, a handsome 18 year old Roman Catholic, who was also her cousin. They had a son who became **James VI of Scotland** and later **James I of England**. The marriage strengthened Mary's claim to the English throne. She and her husband were both grandchildren of Henry VIII's sister Margaret Tudor. Darnley was proclaimed King of Scotland ruling alongside Mary.

Add to your timeline the important dates in Mary's life as related in this unit.

Activity

The murder of Rizzio

Darnley turned out to be lazy, arrogant and spoilt. In 1566 he led a plot to murder **David Rizzio**, the Queen's Italian secretary and musician. Armed men burst into the Queen's apartment and dragged Rizzio screaming into the hall where he was stabbed and hacked to death. The body suffered 56 stab wounds. Darnley was convinced that Rizzio was Mary's secret lover.

The murder of Rizzio (painting by Sir William Allan 1833)

Mary stayed with Darnley until their son James was born, but she had now fallen in love with the Earl of Bothwell, a dashing young soldier. On 9 February 1567 Darnley was lying ill at a house on the outskirts of Edinburgh called Kirk O'Fields. The house was blown up and the body of both Darnley and his servant were found strangled in the garden (Source C). Rumours swept Edinburgh that Bothwell and even the Queen were involved in the murder of Darnley. Despite this, Mary married Bothwell three months later. This led to an immediate rebellion. Mary was captured and imprisoned in Lochleven Castle, and her infant son James was proclaimed James VI. But Mary escaped in May 1568 and arrived in England to throw herself on the mercy of her cousin, **Elizabeth I.**

A print showing Darnley's body at Kirk O'Fields 1567

Questions

1 Source B was painted in 1833, 267 years after the event took place. Is it reliable as evidence? Explain your answer.

2 Why do you think Source C was produced?

3 How may the answer to Question 2 affect the reliability of Source C?

1.7 Mary and Elizabeth I

The arrival of Mary Queen of Scots in England caused major problems for Queen Elizabeth I.

The problem of Mary Queen of Scots

◆ Elizabeth could hardly refuse political sanctuary for her cousin.

◆ Since Elizabeth was unmarried and had no children, Mary was her heir. Elizabeth was 35 and might yet marry, of course.

◆ The French had recognised Mary as Queen of England. Look at the family tree on page 16 again. Because Catholics did not believe Henry VIII was legitimately married to his second wife Anne Boleyn, they regarded Elizabeth as the daughter of his mistress and so not entitled to be Queen. Thus to Catholics, Mary Queen of Scots was the rightful heir of Mary I (Mary Tudor).

◆ If Mary was allowed to live in England unrestricted, English Catholics might be tempted to make Mary Queen and thus rebel against Elizabeth.

◆ Mary's son James was being brought up as a Protestant. If Elizabeth sent Mary back to Scotland it could result in a Catholic Queen north of the border, instead of a Protestant King. Alternatively, the Scots might kill Mary.

◆ If she sent Mary to France, Catholic powers might invade England in an attempt to make Mary Queen.

◆ The easy way out might be to execute Mary – but on what grounds? She had committed no crime in England. In any case if a Queen executed another Queen it might set a precedent.

A

We declare the aforesaid Elizabeth to be excommunicated by the Church. Moreover, we declare that Elizabeth's title as Queen of England is false. No English nobles or subjects need keep their promises of loyalty or obedience to her. No one may obey her orders ....

Extract from the Papal Bull of 1570

Mary Queen of Scots in captivity in England

1 In groups, construct a prosecution and a defence case for Mary Queen of Scots, who is accused of treason. One representative from each group is to put their case to the rest of the class.

2 (a) Write a letter from Mary Queen of Scots to Elizabeth, protesting her innocence and asking for Elizabeth's sympathy and help.

(b) Write a letter from Elizabeth to her most trusted adviser, explaining her dilemma about how to deal with Mary.

Elizabeth was careful never to meet Mary face to face. Instead she had the charges against Mary investigated, but the investigation neither proved Mary guilty of involvement in Darnley's murder, nor innocent either. Mary was allowed to stay in England as a 'guest' of Elizabeth, but in reality she was a prisoner, held at various castles against her will. During this time Mary was the focus of a number of plots against Elizabeth. This was a dangerous time for Elizabeth internationally. Catholic Spain was now an enemy of England, and Elizabeth was secretly aiding Protestants in the Netherlands who were rebelling against Spain. The Pope regarded Elizabeth as a heretic and in 1570 issued a **Papal Bull**. Part of this is reproduced in Source A.

Queen Elizabeth I

sanctuary – a safe place to stay

excommunicated – deprived of any right to the services of the Church and therefore doomed to spend eternity in Hell

precedent – an example that others might copy

Papal Bull – a declaration carrying the full authority of the Church

1 How can we tell from Source A that the threat to Elizabeth I's position from her Catholic subjects would be increased?

2 Why do you think that Elizabeth would never agree to meet Mary?

3 Look at Elizabeth's elaborate clothing in Source B. What does this tell you about Elizabethan society?

Questions

1.8 The death of Mary Queen of Scots

From this time on the number of plots involving Mary increased and in 1572 Parliament brought charges against her (Source A). Below are some of the plots and events of the period.

A

i That she has wickedly and untruly challenged the present estate and possession of the crown of England and ... usurped the style and arms of the same.

ii That she has ... sought by subtle means to withdraw the late Duke of Norfolk from his natural obedience and against Her Majesty's express prohibition to couple herself in marriage with the said Duke, to the intent that thereby she might ... bring to effect Her Majesty's ... destruction.

iii That she has ... stirred ... the Earls of Northumberland and Westmorland ... to rebel and levy open war against Her Majesty.

iv That she has practised ... to procure new rebellion to be raised within this realm. And for that intent she made choice of one Ridolphi, a merchant of Italy, who ... solicited the said wicked enterprises to the Pope and other ... confederates beyond the Seas.

Charges made by Parliament against Mary Queen of Scots in May 1572

1571 Ridolfi Plot. Ridolfi (an Italian) planned to marry Mary to the Duke of Norfolk, and replace Elizabeth with her. In 1572 Norfolk was beheaded.

1572 St Bartholomew's Day Massacre in France. This was begun by the Guises, Mary's French relatives. (See page 11).

1584 Assassination of William of Orange, the Protestant ruler of the Netherlands. This frightened the English government, who wanted Mary to be executed.

Elizabeth could not bring herself to harm Mary, so **Sir Francis Walsingham** (Elizabeth's secretary) set up a trap for her. A young Catholic, **Anthony Babington**, was persuaded to pass secret messages from Mary to a continental 'agent' (who was in fact a spy for Walsingham). The code for the messages is shown in Source B. When the trap was sprung there was enough proof to find both Babington and Mary Queen of Scots guilty of treason.

Mary was tried in October 1586 at **Fotheringay Castle**, but it was February 1587 before Elizabeth was persuaded to sign the death warrant. The execution took place on 8 February at Fotheringay. Source D is a contemporary account of the event.

B

a	b	c	d	e	f	g	h	i	k	l	m
o	‡	△	⧻	a	□	⊕	∞	ı	ð	n	//

n	o	p	q	r	s	t	u	x	y	z
ø	▽	s	m	ʄ	△	Ɛ	c	7	8	9

One of the codes used in the Babington plot

A contemporary drawing of the execution of Mary Queen of Scots, February 1587

D

With a smiling face she turned to her men servants standing upon a bench (behind the platform). They were weeping. The Queen bid them farewell.

She kneeled down upon a cushion and prayed. Then, groping for the block with both her hands, she held them there. They would have been cut off had they not been espied (seen). Then she laid herself upon the block, most quietly. It took two strokes of the axe before he (the executioner) cut off her head. Then one espied a little dog which was under the (dead queen's) clothes. It could not be gotten out by force and afterwards would not depart the dead corpse but came and laid by the shoulders.

A contemporary account of the execution of Mary Queen of Scots, written by Robert Wyngfield

Activity

Use the code in Source B to compose a short letter from Babington's continental 'agent', trying to encourage Mary to take part in a plot against Elizabeth.

Questions

1 Rank in order of importance the charges made by Parliament against Mary Queen of Scots in May 1572 (Source A). Give reasons for the order you have chosen.

2 Why did Elizabeth's attitude to Mary change after 1572?

3 What are the similarities between the two accounts of Mary's execution (Sources C and D)?

4 Account for any differences in the two versions.

1.9 England and Spain

Queen Elizabeth knighting Sir Francis Drake (after the original by the Victorian artist Gilbert)

By 1588 England had become one of the greatest naval powers in the world. This in itself was enough to make England and Spain bitter rivals in the second half of the sixteenth century. The early voyages of discovery to Africa, Asia and the New World (America) had been by Portuguese and Spanish seamen. **Columbus**, who reached America in 1492, was financed by Spain, though Italian himself. In 1494 Spain and Portugal had signed a treaty dividing the New World between them. The New World had abundant resources of silver and gold and soon made Spain rich.

After 1550 England began to get in on the act. English seamen began to trade with both west Africa and south America. At first this was peaceful, but in 1567 a Spanish fleet attacked English ships, commanded by **Sir John Hawkins** in San Juan de Ulua harbour in Mexico. Henceforth English seamen regarded Spain as an enemy.

Whilst in Europe the two governments remained officially at peace, piracy became the order of the day on the high seas. The most famous pirate was **Sir Francis Drake** who, in the ***Golden Hind***, sailed round the world in 1577–80. On this voyage he captured the treasure ship *Cacafuego* loaded with 26 tons of silver, 360 000 pieces of eight (gold) and expensive cloth. When Drake got home, the Queen received a 'cut' of the loot and Drake was knighted. When the Spanish Ambassador protested to Elizabeth, she denied any knowledge of the event, but it was said at the time that as she was talking to him, the royal dressmaker was measuring her for a new dress in Spanish cloth of gold, stolen on the voyage!

Spain and the Netherlands

Philip II, King of Spain had inherited the Netherlands from his father Emperor Charles V in 1555. The Netherlands, sometimes known as Flanders, was wealthy because of the wool trade and cloth making. Flemish merchants had become rich through this trade. Philip II lived in the Netherlands until 1559, when he moved to Spain. Around the same time militant Protestantism was spreading in the Netherlands. A revolt against the rule of Philip II began in 1567. This had four main causes which you can read in the box on the right.

England and the Netherlands

At first England gave only indirect help to the Netherlands. Elizabeth was anxious to avoid full scale war with Spain. She saw France as a bigger danger to England. However, a Spanish victory in the Netherlands would have threatened England's own cloth trade, as well as removing a potential Protestant ally. In 1584 William the Silent was assassinated, and in 1585 Antwerp, an important port, fell to the Spanish. Elizabeth sent English troops to help the Dutch. Their arrival, in 1586, helped Philip II make up his mind to invade England.

A modern replica of Drake's *Golden Hind*

Causes of the revolt in the Netherlands

◆ Philip II wanted to remove many of the privileges of the 17 provinces of the Netherlands, and govern them directly from Brussels.

◆ Philip wanted to stamp out Protestantism in the Netherlands, and introduced the Jesuits and the Inquisition. He began burning Protestants at the stake. This also antagonised Flemish Catholics who were tolerant and did not want persecution. In 1566 Protestants rioted, wrecking Catholic churches.

◆ In 1567 Philip sent a large army to the Netherlands in a show of force, designed to quell opposition. This army began a reign of terror in Flanders.

◆ The Spanish government imposed heavy taxes on the Netherlands to pay for this army.

1 List all the reasons why Philip II of Spain may have been annoyed with Elizabeth I and England at this time.

2 Which of these reasons do you think is the most important? Give your reasons.

Questions

1.10   Philip II

Phillip II of Spain and Mary I of England

Philip II had been keeping an eye on England for a long time. Spain and England had been allies in the time of Henry VII (1485–1509) and Henry VIII (1509–1547), but this had weakened with the Protestant Reformation in England in the reign of Edward VI (1547–53). However the accession of Mary 1 (1553–58), a Catholic, returned England to the Spanish camp. Philip II married Mary, and if the marriage had not been childless, England could have become part of the Spanish Empire. Mary's death in 1558 ended any such hopes since her younger sister Elizabeth I (1558–1603) was a Protestant. Philip asked Elizabeth to marry him, but she refused.

Philip was convinced that the people of England were Catholic at heart, and he planned to overthrow Elizabeth and replace her with a Catholic monarch – perhaps Mary Queen of Scots. The Spanish ambassador to England kept a close eye on the persecution of English Catholics and reported back to Philip regularly as these extracts in Sources A, B and C show.

C

In accordance with the laws which I said had been passed in this parliament, they have begun to persecute the Catholics worse than ever before, both by condemning them to the £20 fine if they do not attend church every month and by imprisoning them closely in the gaols. The clergymen they succeed in capturing are treated with a variety of terrible tortures: amongst others is one torment that people in Spain imagine to be that which will be worked by Anti-Christ as the most dreadfully cruel of them all. This is to drive iron spikes between the nails and the quick; and two clergymen in the tower have been tortured in this way, one of them being Campion of the Company of Jesus, who, with the other was recently captured. I am assured that when they would not confess under this torture the nails of their fingers and toes were turned back; all of which they suffered with great patience and humility.

Spanish Ambassador to Philip II, 12 August 1581

D

You will cautiously approach his Holiness (the Pope) and in such terms as you think fit endeavour to obtain from him a secret brief declaring that, failing the Queen of Scotland, the right to the English Crown falls to me ... You will impress upon his Holiness that I cannot undertake a war in England for the purpose merely of placing upon that throne a young heretic like the King of Scotland (James VI) who, indeed, is by his heresy incapacitated to succeed. His Holiness must, however, be assured that I have no intention of adding England to my own dominions, but to settle the crown upon my daughter, the Infanta.

Philip II to his Ambassador in Rome, 11 February 1587

Philip and the Pope

Philip had been pressing the Pope for some time to give his blessing to a Spanish invasion of England. Philip claimed that if Spanish troops landed, thousands of Englishmen would flock to their support. The Pope was not so sure. He was reluctant to offend Philip who was one of the foremost champions of the Catholic faith in Europe, but he suspected that Philip might have other motives, as well as a religious crusade, to overthrow Protestantism in England. The Pope did not want the power of Spain to get any greater.

Despite his doubts the Pope eventually felt he had no choice but to approve and bless Philip's invasion plan.

Sixteenth-century torture

1. What are the strengths and weaknesses of using only the Spanish ambassador's accounts of the treatment of English Catholics?
(Sources A, B and C)

2. Why do you think the Pope gave his approval to Philip's plan to attack England?

3. How does the evidence in Sources C and E illustrate the cruelty which appears to be common in sixteenth-century Europe?

4. What sentence in Source D suggests that Philip II is anxious to dispel the Pope's suspicions?

5. Mary Queen of Scots had been executed on 8 February 1587, three days before Source D was written. What words in the letter suggest that this news had not yet reached Philip?

25

1.11 The Armada's voyage

At first Philip planned to send a huge army to England direct from Spain, but this would have required 500 ships and would have been much too costly. So Philip fell back on a cheaper plan. This plan was to use the Spanish army in the Netherlands to invade England. These could be conveyed in flat barges which would be towed across the English channel. They would be protected by a much smaller fleet of warships and supply ships that would sail from Spain to accompany them.

These plans were frustrated by bad luck and by English military action.

In groups or with a partner list the advantages and disadvantages of sending an Armada to attack Britain in 1588. What advice would you give Philip II?

◆ In April 1587 Drake raided Cadiz and destroyed 24 big Spanish ships, as well as supply ships.

◆ Several supply ships carrying barrel staves (intended for the barrels carrying food for the Armada) were captured. Later the Armada was to suffer from barrels made of unseasoned wood which made the food and water go rotten.

◆ Early in 1588 the commander of the Armada, Santa Cruz, died. His replacement, chosen for rank rather than experience, was the **Duke of Medina Sidonia** who had little knowledge of the sea.

◆ The Spanish failed to capture a port in the Netherlands with deep enough water to accommodate the Armada.

A

We whose names are hereunder written, have determined and agreed in council to follow and pursue the Spanish fleet until we have cleared our own coast and brought the firth west of us, and then to return back again, as well to restock our ships (which stand in extreme supplies) as also to guard and defend our own coast at home; with further protestation that, if our lack of food and munitions were supplied, we would pursue them to the furthest they have gone.

The Resolution of the Council of War of the English Commanders to fight against the Armada, 1 August 1588

The Armada sails

On **20 May 1588** the Armada set sail from Lisbon in Portugal. It consisted of 130 ships, drawn from all parts of the Spanish Empire, including rowing galleys from the eastern Mediterranean. The fleet was made up of 75 fighting ships, 25 large merchant ships, and 30 small sloops. They carried 10,000 sailors, 20,000 soldiers and over 2000 artillery pieces. In contrast the English could muster 102 warships, though only 25 were first line ships. The progress of the Armada is summarised in the timeline.

Timeline of the Armada

20 May
Set sail from Lisbon.

9 June
Fleet dispersed by storm off Corunna. Month's delay to regroup.

19 July
English sighted the Armada off Cornwall. Beacon fires relayed the news to Plymouth and London.

19-27 July
Nine days battle up the English channel. The Armada adopted a crescent formation with the English attacking from behind.

27 July
Spanish fleet anchored off Calais hoping for a week to take on fresh supplies.

28 July
Armada attacked in darkness by eight fireships (each English commander had given up his oldest ship). In panic many of the Spanish cut their anchors and headed out to sea.

29 July-3 Aug
Six day battle off the Kent coast. Several Spanish ships were sunk. The Spanish could not reach the Netherlands, land in England or regroup. They headed into the North Sea. Both sides ran low in ammunition and near the Scottish coast the English turned back.

Aug-Oct
Spanish fleet passed round Scotland and Ireland but was badly damaged by storm and high seas. At least 19 ships were wrecked off the Irish coast. Others were driven out into the Atlantic and foundered.

barrel staves – strips of wood from which a barrel is made

founder – sink by taking on water

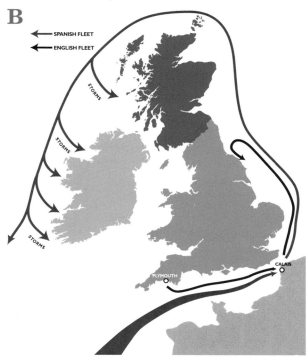

B

SPANISH FLEET

ENGLISH FLEET

STORMS

PLYMOUTH

CALAIS

The route of the Armada

About a third of the ships were sunk. Another third were so badly damaged that they could never sail again. Medina Sidonia finally got back on 23 October, delirious from lack of water. A third of the men did not return.

1 **Put the following reasons for the failure of the Spanish Armada in order of importance.**
   a) **Attack by English fire ships at Calais on 28 July**
   b) **Storms off Ireland and Scotland from August to October**
   c) **Rotten food on board the Spanish ships**
   d) **The death of Santa Cruz, the Spanish Admiral**
   e) **The battle formation of the Spanish fleet**
   f) **Spanish shortage of ammunition**
   g) **The Spanish had poor maps**
   h) **Drake's attack on Cadiz in 1587**
   i) **Failure of the Spanish to get a deep water port in the Netherlands**
   j) **The tactics adopted by the English fleet**

2 **What would (i) Philip II and (ii) Elizabeth I have regarded as the most important reasons?**

1.12 Ireland and the Armada

A

A sixteenth-century map of Ireland similar to the maps used by the Spanish

B

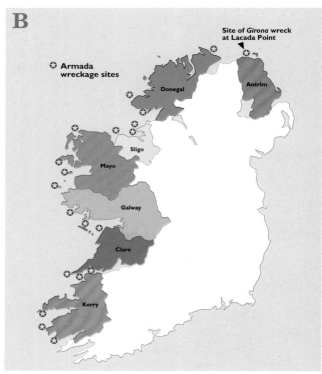

Ireland as it is in reality. The seven counties with Armada wrecks are marked.

C

Irish Armada wrecks 1588

Ship	Ton	Soldiers	Sailors	Rowers	Guns	Wrecksite	Date
San Marcos	790	292	117	0	33	Clare	20 Sep
La Lavia	728	203	71	0	25	Sligo	25 Sep
La Rata Encoronada	820	335	84	0	35	Mayo	21 Sep
La Trinidad Valencera	1100	281	79	0	42	Donegal	16 Sep
La Anunciada	703	196	79	0	24	Clare	20 Sep
San Nicolas Prodaneli	834	274	81	0	26	Mayo	16 Sep
Juliana	860	325	70	0	32	Donegal	?
Santa Maria De Vision	666	236	71	0	18	Sligo	25 Sep
San Juan	530	163	113	0	24	Sligo	25 Sep
La Trinidad	872	180	122	0	24	Kerry	15 Sep
San Juan Bautista	652	192	93	0	24	Kerry	24 Sep
Girona	700	169	120	300	50	Antrim	28 Oct
El Gran Grin	1160	256	73	0	28	Clare	22 Sep
Urca Duquesa Santa Ana	900	280	77	0	23	Donegal	26 Sep
Santa Maria De La Rosa	945	225	64	0	0	Kerry	21 Sep
San Esteban	936	196	68	0	26	Clare	20 Sep
Falcon Blanco Mediano	300	76	27	0	16	Galway	25 Sep
Ciervo Volante	400	200	22	0	18	Mayo	22 Sep
Santiago	600	56	30	0	19	Mayo	21 Sep

D

Some of the Armada ships getting ready to sail

Why were so many Spanish ships wrecked off the west coast of Ireland? Let us go back to what happened at Calais. When the fireships approached the Armada on 28 July, the Spanish ships had cut their anchors. Most ships had at least one spare anchor, but if a ship is being carried towards land by an onshore storm, such as the Armada faced off Ireland in September, it will drop anchor to avoid shipwreck. But the ships no longer had enough anchors!

The second factor is that the Spanish thought Ireland looked like the map in Source A. They assumed that if you sailed round the top of Ireland heading west, you could turn south about ten miles past Donegal. But in reality, if you did that, you would find Sligo and Mayo in the way! With the wind direction SW they could not get back out to sea again. Ten of the nineteen wrecks were off Mayo, Sligo and Donegal. Those Spaniards who did make it ashore found themselves robbed, stripped, beaten and sometimes killed by the local Irish people.

Questions

1 A galley was a ship which had oars and rowers. Study Source C. Which Armada wreck was a galley?

2 List the five largest Armada wrecks.

3 In what ways was the information in Source A unreliable?

4 How useful is Source A in helping us to understand why so many Spanish ships were lost around the Irish coast?

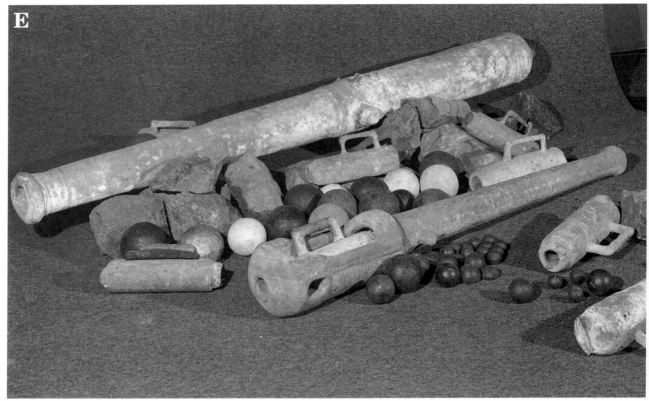

E

The Girona

The most famous Armada wreck was that of the ***Girona***. The *Girona* had managed to find refuge at Killybegs in Donegal, and had been joined there by the crew of two wrecked ships – *Santa Maria Encoronada* and *Duquessa Santa Ana*. The *Girona*'s captain decided to over-winter in Scotland and was heading east along the North Antrim coast when his ship was wrecked on 28 October at Lacada Point near the Giant's Causeway. Of the 1,300 on board five survived.

In 1967 the wreckage of the *Girona* was located and divers salvaged hundreds of artifacts including cannon, an anchor, gold chains and jewellery. The ship itself had completely disappeared. The *Girona* treasure is now in the Ulster Museum in Belfast.

ordnance – weapons

Ordnance from the *Girona*. The large canon is a bronze half-baker; the smaller one is a bronze esmeril (swivel gun) containing a breech block. Around them are bronze breech blocks and different sizes of stone and iron shot.

F

I passed many Spaniards completely naked without any clothes at all, shivering with the cold that was very severe. The night came upon me in this dreary place and I lay down on some rushes ... a gentleman came up to me, naked, a very gentle youth. He was so frightened that he could not speak, not even to tell me who he was.

Francisco de Cuellar

G

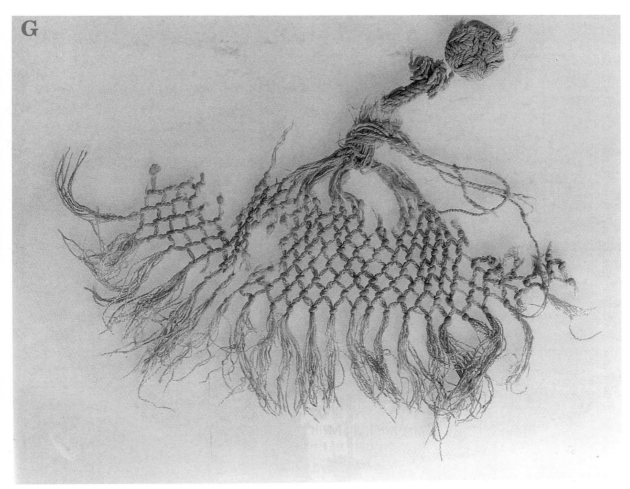

Silk tassel from *La Trinidad Valencera*

H

At daybreak I began to go towards a monastery ... but found it torn down, the church and holy images burnt and twelve Spaniards hanged within the Church by English Protestants who went about looking for us in order to kill all those who had escaped the hazard of the sea. I found nobody there except the Spaniards dangling from the iron grills in the church windows ... I went out very quickly.

Francisco de Cuellar

The end of the war

The war between England and Spain continued after 1588, but the Armada was its climax. In **1598** Philip II died and in **1603** Elizabeth I died. Her successor, James I made peace with Spain in **1604**.

Questions

5 Sources F and H were written by a Spaniard, therefore they must be unreliable. Explain why you agree or disagree with this.

6 Of what use is it for a historian to have pictures of the wrecked ship *Girona* and its contents?

2.1   What is a colony?

A colony can be defined as:
a settlement in a new country, forming a community which is either partly or fully subject to the mother state.

In the fifthteenth and sixteenth centuries, many European countries established colonies in various parts of the world, especially in those areas which are now known as the Americas. Soon these Spanish and Portuguese explorers were followed by **Conquistadors** (Conquerors). They discovered ancient but advanced civilisations such as the **Aztecs** of Mexico and the **Incas** of Peru. These colonies in South America had huge quantities of gold and silver which were sent back to Europe in treasure ships.

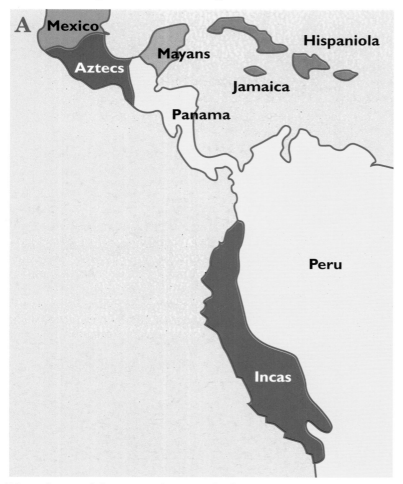

Map of central America, showing the location of the Inca and Aztec civilisations

A

If our nation were once planted in North America, or near thereabouts; whereas (English fishing boats) now fish but for two months of the year, they might then fish so long as pleased themselves.

Hakluyt: *Principal Navigations* Vol VIII, 1598–1600

C

... it is well known that all Savages ... as soon as they shall begin but a little to taste of civility, will take marvellous delight in any garment, be it never so simple; as a shirt, a blue, yellow, red or green cotton cassock, a cap, or such like, and will take incredible pains for such a trifle ... how great benefit to all Clothiers, Woolmen, Carders, Spinners, Weavers, Fullers etc would be the establishment of colonies in America and Far East.

Hakluyt: *Principal Navigations* Vol VIII, 1598–1600

Many English people believed that they too should seek colonies in North America.

Study the Sources B, C, D and E and answer the questions opposite.

D

... this voyage is not altogether undertaken for ourselves but ... the Savages shall have cause to bless the hour when this enterprise was undertaken.

First and Chiefly, in respect of the most happy and gladsome tidings of the most glorious gospel of our Saviour, Jesus Christ, whereby they may be brought from falsehood to truth ...

... being brought from brutish ignorance to civility and knowledge, they may be taught how one tenth of their land, if manured and ploughed, would yield as much as the whole presently does ...

But this is not all the benefit which they shall receive: for over and beside the knowledge how to till and dress their grounds, they shall be reduced from unseemly customs to honest manners, from disordered riotous routs to a well governed Commonwealth ...

Hakluyt: *Principal Navigations* Vol VIII, 1598–1600

E

It will prove a general benefit unto our country that, not only a great number of men which do now live idly at home and are a burden, chargeable and unprofitable to this realm, shall hereby be set to work, but also children of twelve and fourteen years of age or older, may be kept from idleness, in making of a thousand kinds of trifling things which will be good merchandise for that country and, moreover, our idle women shall also be employed on plucking, drying, and sorting of feathers, in pulling, beating and working of hemp, and in gathering of cotton, and diverse things for dyeing.

Hakluyt: *Principal Navigations* Vol VIII, 1598–1600

Questions

1. What do Sources B, C, D and E tell you about the English view of the natives of North America?
2. Which source would most appeal to an English wool merchant? Give reasons for your answer.
3. To which group would Source D be addressed?
4. List the reasons given in all four sources for England to have colonies in North America.
5. List these reasons in rank order from the point of view of (a) a merchant/trader and (b) an Anglican bishop.
6. Suggest reasons why the rank orders may differ from each other.
7. Sources B, C, D and E came from the same book. What does this tell us about its author, Hakluyt?

An artist's impression of explorers arriving in the New World

2.2 Colonies and trade

Trading links were important reasons for setting up colonies abroad (see Sources A and B). Improved navigation techniques meant that much longer voyages could be undertaken by adventurous sailors.

New areas were conquered all over the known world and, of course, each area had something valuable to be exploited by the European countries. Some of these goods were spices to enhance food and cooking. Others included tobacco and dyes but the sixteenth century also saw the beginning of the slave trade. This normally took the form of capturing natives on the west coast of Africa and taking them to America where they were sold as slaves.

During this period some trade journeys were made partially over land, such as the silk route to and from China and cottons from India.

A

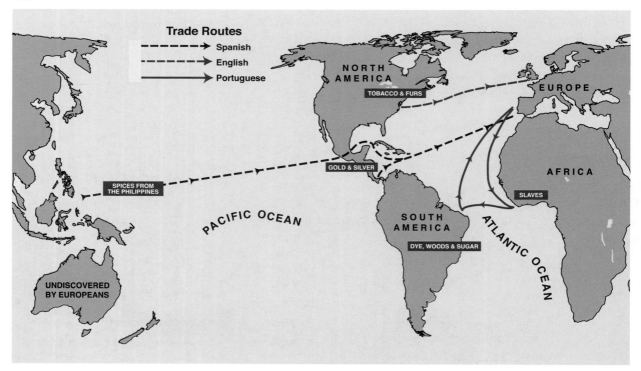

Sixteenth-century trade between Europe, Africa and the Americas

B

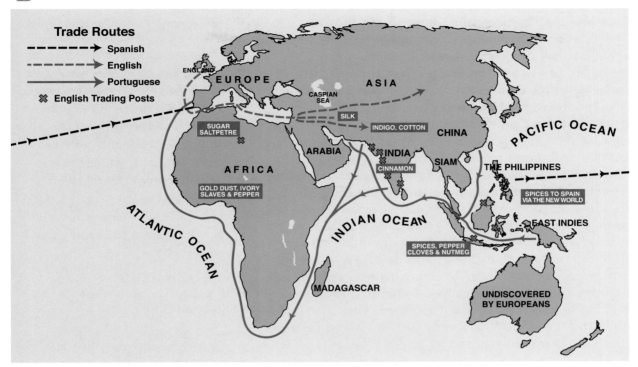

Trade Routes
- - - - → Spanish
- - - - → English
——→ Portuguese
✳ English Trading Posts

ENGLAND
EUROPE
ASIA
CASPIAN SEA
SILK
SUGAR SALTPETRE
INDIGO, COTTON
CHINA
PACIFIC OCEAN
ARABIA
AFRICA
INDIA
CINNAMON
SIAM
THE PHILIPPINES
GOLD DUST, IVORY SLAVES & PEPPER
SPICES TO SPAIN VIA THE NEW WORLD
ATLANTIC OCEAN
INDIAN OCEAN
EAST INDIES
SPICES, PEPPER CLOVES & NUTMEG
MADAGASCAR
UNDISCOVERED BY EUROPEANS

Sixteenth-century trade between Europe, Africa, India and the Far East during Elizabeth's reign

C

For 4000 gold pesos from the King's treasure Castellanos (Philip's treasurer) acquired 60 Negroes and with 1000 pesos of his own money ... a further 20, then trade was open to all ... Admiral [John Hawkins] and treasurer now exchanged rich presents and gave the appearance of becoming warm friends ... In his official report to Spain Castellanos wove an ingenious yarn that the 4000 pesos of royal money had been used to pay a ransom for what still stood of the town, including the church.

From *The Sea Dogs* by Neville Williams, London, 1975

Questions

1 Using Source A, list the goods received by England, Spain and Portugal from the Americas.

2 Which country do you think would become richest from this trade alone, and why do you think this is the case?

3 Study the English trade routes in Source B. Suggest ways in which English goods were transported from India to England.

4 What problems may these routes have caused?

5 What additional evidence would be needed to give a fuller picture of the trading links between the colonies and Europe in the sixteenth century?

6 Suggest why Castellanos' own slaves were cheaper.

7 How can we tell from Source C that the Spanish King did not approve of this slave trading?

2.3　The American colonies

In 1606, the English King, James I, granted permission to the London Virginia Company to take control of a large area of land in Virginia. They hoped to discover gold and silver there. This colony was called **Jamestown**. One of the pioneers was called **John Smith**. The colonists sailed in three ships: *Discovery*, *Susan Constant*, and *God Speed*. They reached Chesapeake Bay in April 1607 and saw meadows, trees, and fresh waters.

The Indians were friendly at first. The first thing the new settlers did was to choose a site and the London Company had given specific instructions about this. Jamestown, which the colonists built, did not fulfil all the requirements but was the best site they could find. They built a fort there so that they would be safe if attacked. The next urgent tasks were to clear the ground, to make temporary houses for themselves, to plant vegetables, and to make nets for catching their food. They also had to start filling the ships with a cargo to take home, because the London Company wanted its profit.

John Smith

Before leaving England, the names of those chosen by the London Virginia Company to govern the colony were put in a locked box. This was opened when they reached America, and one of the seven names was John Smith who was an army captain. However, he had quarrelled so much with the others that he was not made a council member. Later (in May) the native Indians became unfriendly and raided the colony so Smith was asked to help the colonists defend Jamestown.

Smith believed that the colonists needed to be made to work. He said, "If you do not work, you shall not eat". He took command (see Source B).

By September 1607 half of the original 104 settlers were dead from malaria or typhoid. As those who survived were very weak, it was even more necessary to build defences (see Source A).

A

There were never Englishmen left in a foreign country in such misery as we were in this new discovered Virginia. We watched every three nights, lying on the bare cold ground, what weather so ever came; warded (guarded) all the next day; which brought our men to be most feeble wretches, not having five able men to man our bulwarks (strong defences) upon any occasion.

From *Captain John Smith and Virginia* (Then and There series, Longman 1968)

B

... by his own example, good words, and fair promises set some to mow, others to bind thatch; some to build houses, others to thatch them; himself always bearing the greatest task for his own share; so that, in short time, he provided most of them lodgings, neglecting any for himself.

From *Captain John Smith and Virginia* (Then and There series, Longman 1968)

Artist's impression of the original Jamestown colony

Pocahontas

The most pressing problem was shortage of food. Until they could grow their own crops, they had to trade with the Indians. They gave the Indians beads, copper and hatchets in return for bread, venison, turkeys and wild fowl. On one of these expeditions Smith was captured by some Indians who were going to kill him by beating his brains out. What happened next is related in Source C.

Smith returned to his colony and was made President on 10 September 1608. He extended the fort, tightened the discipline of the colonists and trained military units. Cargo was still being sent to England where merchants were looking for pitch, tar, soap-ashes and cut wood. Smith was bitter, because these things were not abundant in Virginia where the colonists were struggling to live. Colonists now were very disgruntled, but Smith kept them together, mainly because they were impressed by his exploits.

C

Pocahontas, the King's dearest daughter, when no entreaty could prevail, got his head in her arms, and laid her own upon his to save him from death: whereat the King was contented he should live to make him hatchets, and her bells, beads and copper; for they thought him as well of all other occupations as them-selves, for the King himself will make his own robes, shoes, bows, arrows, pots.

From *Captain John Smith and Virginia* (Then and There series, Longman 1968)

Pocahontas, who married Englishman John Rolfe. She came to England with him but died in 1617, aged only 22.

Activity

When John Smith returned to London, people in Virginia were left with mixed feelings about him. Form groups. Half of the groups prepare speeches defending the actions of John Smith; the other half condemning him.
Representatives of these groups may present their evidence to a tribunal which, on the basis of this evidence, decides John Smith's fate.

Questions

List the various problems which faced these early settlers.

Smith leaves Virginia

In July 1609 a ship left England carrying vital supplies, but also letters criticising Smith for not sending back enough goods. Some great men in England decided to govern Virginia, and Smith returned to London.

The colony grew gradually, but Indian massacres in 1622 and 1644 affected the flow of settlers. Eventually, the Indians were defeated by the better weapons of the colonists. A new town was built further inland, away from the unhealthy swamps, and great plantations developed using negro slaves.

2.4　Ireland before the Plantations

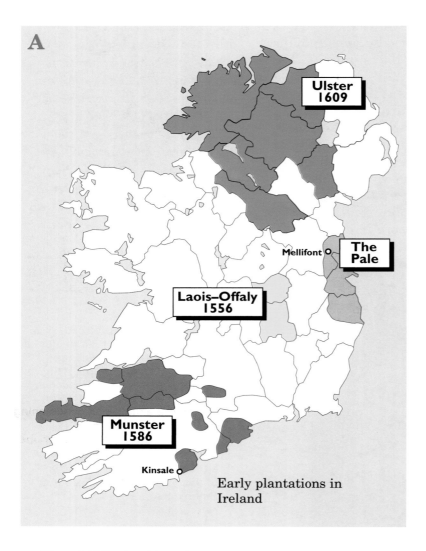

A

Ulster
1609

Mellifont ○

The
Pale

Laois–Offaly
1556

Munster
1586

Kinsale ○

Early plantations in
Ireland

The English King was represented in Ireland by a Viceroy who was assisted by a Chief Secretary. Until the middle of the sixteenth century, the English could extend their control only over the area around Dublin, known as **The Pale**. Areas outside this paid little attention to English rule and were regarded as being "beyond the Pale".

The English faced many problems in Ireland, but from the middle of the sixteenth century they had gradually extended their control over Ireland. One method which they used was the establishment of plantations, where English and Scottish planters or settlers had come to live and work in Ireland. Early plantation schemes were carried out in Laois, Offaly and in Munster.

There were also plantations in Ards, Co Down (1570) and Antrim (1573). There was always the likelihood of trouble in Ireland in spite of English attempts to control the area.

Reasons for Plantation

◆ The Irish chiefs looked to Spain for help during a rebellion by the Desmonds in Munster.
◆ The English feared that Spain might attack them via Ireland.
◆ There was a view that a barbarous country must first be broken by war before it will be capable of good government.
◆ The Irish remained Catholic, Gaelic and used their own laws. England was not happy with this.
◆ The only area ruled directly by the English was The Pale, a district round Dublin. This was the only foothold for English rule in Ireland.
◆ Henry VIII, the Protestant King of England, took the title 'King of Ireland'. Tudor governments tried to make all Ireland obey English law.

Form groups. Compose a speech to be delivered to the English Parliament in 1608. Half of the groups state the benefits of Plantation in Ireland. The other half express objections.

Dolose agunt fily iniquitatis

Hugh O'Neill, on the left, coming to parley with the English Commander before battle

The Nine Years' War

After 1594 some of the most important Irish clans had gone to war against the forces of Queen Elizabeth. They were led by Hugh O'Neill who was also known as the Earl of Tyrone.

The Irish claimed that they were fighting to preserve their old way of life which was being threatened by English rule. This old way of life meant the Irish system of laws and the Roman Catholic faith. For some years they were successful, but on 24 December 1601 Irish forces were defeated at the **Battle of Kinsale**. Although O'Neill came back to Tyrone with his army, he knew that he had little chance of success against the English.

During 1602 the English strengthened their forts around O'Neill's territory in Tyrone. Lord Mountjoy ordered crops and cattle to be destroyed so the Irish would be starved into submission.

In the same year, one of O'Neill's allies, the head of the O'Cahan clan, made peace with the English. O'Neill still refused to surrender. The English decided to make peace as the war had proved very costly. So the **Treaty of Mellifont** was signed in **1603**. O'Neill gave up his Irish title and accepted English laws. In return he was allowed to keep his lands.

Many of the English who had fought in Ulster saw how prosperous a land it could be and they were prepared to take a chance to live there.

1 Which of the reasons for Plantation support these statements:
(a) England was worried about foreign enemies
(b) Religious differences were seen as a problem
(c) England wished to extend control over Ireland?

2 Which of these reasons do you think was the most important? Give reasons for your answer.

3 When O'Neill signed the Treaty of Mellifont, he had not heard that Elizabeth had died. How might this have affected his decision to sign?

parley – to discuss terms with an enemy

39

2.5 Plantation

A replica Plantation House, Ulster History Park, Omagh, Co Tyrone

When Elizabeth died in 1603 she was succeeded by her nearest relative, the son of Mary Queen of Scots, **James VI of Scotland** who became **James I** of England.

The Nine Years' War had again shown the English just how vulnerable they could be to attack from Ireland. This was especially worrying as the Spanish were still smarting after the defeat of their famous Armada.

Many believed that Spain could use Ireland as a possible base from which to attack England. For this reason it became very important to king and government to find a way of controlling the rebel province of Ulster.

Officials in London believed that as long as Catholics held land, they could raise the men and equipment necessary to stage a rebellion. Consequently, the English decided to plant colonies with loyal Protestants, giving them land and support in order that they could survive.

B

Sure it is a most beautiful sweet country as any under heaven ... adorned with goodly woods fit for building houses and ships, full of good ports and havens ... beside the soil itself is most fertile fit to yield all kinds of fruit ... and lastly the heaven most mild and temperate.

Edmund Spenser, Description of Munster, 1580

Activity

Rank order the reasons for supporting a plantation in Ulster from the point of view of an Englishman.

40

C

Art thou a tradesman, a smith, a weaver? Go to Ireland. Thou shall be higher in estimation and quickly enriched.

Art thou a (farmer) whose worth is not past ten or twenty pounds? Go thither. Thou shall whistle sweetly and feed thy whole family if they be six, for sixpence a day.

Art thou a minister of God's word? Make speed ... Thou shalt there see the poor ignorant untaught people worship stones and sticks. Thou, by carrying millions to heaven, may be made an archangel.

From *A Direction for the Plantation in Ulster* by Thomas Blenerhasset, Fermanagh, 1610

D

1 The securing of that wilde Countrye to the Crowne of England.

2 The withdrawing of all the charge of the Garrison and men of warre.

3 The rewarding of the olde servitors to their good content.

4 The meanes how to increase the revenue to the Crowne with a yearly very great somme.

5 How to establish the Purite of Religion there.

6 And how the undertakers may with securite be inriched.

Principal aims of the Plantation given in *A Direction for the Plantation in Ulster* by Thomas Blenerhasset, Fermanagh, 1610

English expectations of Plantation

(a) Ports develop as trade expands.

(b) New towns grow at Cookstown, Strabane, Letterkenny, Londonderry and Coleraine.

(c) English and Scottish planters move in.

(d) Munster has good land. Catholic populations would be driven to poor land in the west of the country. Former land owners are now tenants or labourers.

(e) English soldiers and government officials buy cheap land in Ireland.

(f) Hopefully, a plantation of English and loyal Irish would end threats of rebellion.

1 What kind of settlers would Source C attract to come to Ulster?

2 How can you tell from their expectations that the English government had high hopes for the success of the plantation scheme? (See left.)

uestions

41

2.6 The Ulster Plantation

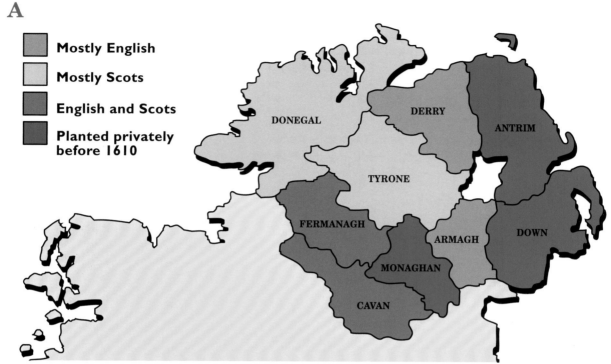

A

- Mostly English
- Mostly Scots
- English and Scots
- Planted privately before 1610

DONEGAL · DERRY · ANTRIM · TYRONE · FERMANAGH · ARMAGH · DOWN · MONAGHAN · CAVAN

The Province of Ulster, showing the counties planted in 1610

After the defeat of O'Neill in Ulster, O'Neill and some other northern chiefs fled from Lough Swilly in 1607 in what has become known as the **Flight of the Earls**. The Irish Lord Deputy, Sir Arthur Chichester, was convinced that the only way to control Ulster was to plant it with English and Scottish settlers. Chichester himself colonised land around Belfast.

In 1609 a number of commissioners travelled the area, mapping the land and finding out who the owners were. They also decided which land belonged to the Church of Ireland, because it was not to be confiscated. If people could not prove their ownership of land, it was usually taken from them.

About four million acres were involved in the scheme, but much of this was not very good land. Some lessons had been learned from earlier plantations. Settlers were not to live in scattered houses, but in fortified villages and towns.

A number of new towns were built by the settlers. The London Companies planted the town of Derry and the surrounding county, renaming it Londonderry.

Activity

If you are familiar with Londonderry or another plantation town as it is today, see if you can trace the town centre and the road or street patterns.

Questions

1 What does Source B tell us about the town planning of these settlers?

2 What other evidence would you need to have if you wished to prove that all the plantation towns followed this pattern?

3 How may the Loyal Irish have been viewed by (a) other Irish people and (b) the new planters?

4 What difficulties did this pose for them?

B

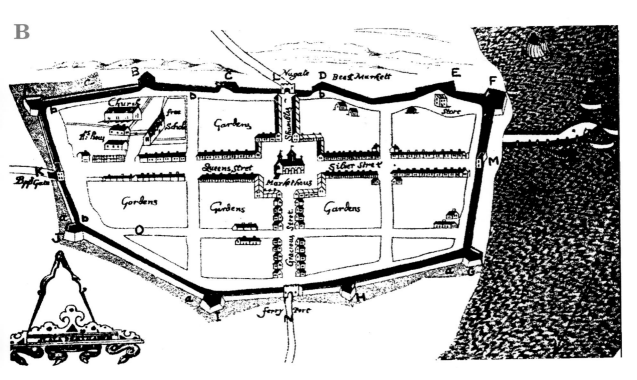

Map of Derry, 1625

Land was granted to:

1 English and Scottish undertakers

- undertook to bring only English and Scottish tenants;
- to build fortifications according to land granted:
  1,000 acres – build a bawn.
  1,500 acres or more – build a bawn and castle.
- tenants to live near bawn and keep arms in readiness.

2 Servitors

- had served the crown in Ireland;
- could have Irish tenants;
- same fortifications as the undertakers.

3 Loyal Irish

- received a tenth of the plantation land;
- same terms as Servitors;
- must use English farming methods.

4 Guilds

- mainly from London and had been involved in Virginia plantations.
- Irish society established to look after Co Londonderry for them as they were usually absentees.

5 Others

- Church of Ireland.
- Trinity College, Dublin.
- Six free schools.

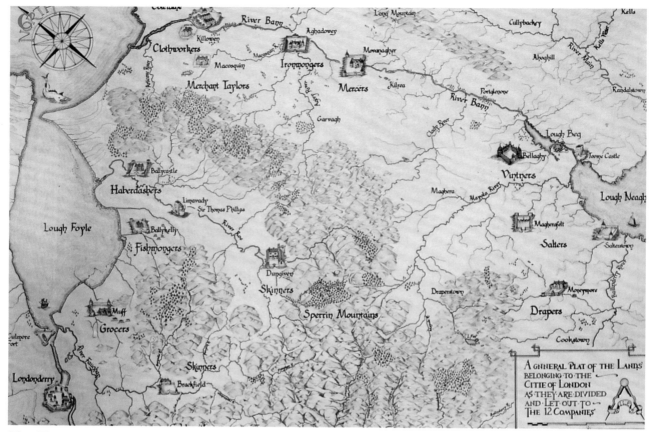

The Plantation in Co Londonderry

A replica plantation bawn at the Ulster History Park, Omagh, Co Tyrone

5 What do the bawns in Source C have in common and how do they differ?

6 Find the meaning of
(a) merchant taylor
(b) skinner
(c) vintner
(d) salter

7 What do the names in Question 6 and the other names in Source C suggest about the people who built these bawns?

8 Describe the sites of these bawns (clue: mountains, rivers).

44

E

Study the artist's impression of Monea Castle and the picture of Clonony keep and bawn. In what ways do they appear to differ? (Clues: shape, windows, roof area.) The stepped gables of Monea are typical of seventeenth-century Scottish architecture. What does it tell you about Monea and Clonony?

Above: An artist's impression of Monea Castle, Co Fermanagh

Clonony Castle,
Co Offaly
Above: the keep
Right: exterior of
the bawn wall

2.7 Omagh – a Plantation case study

In 1602 O'Neill was defeated by Lord Mountjoy at Omagh as the Nine Years' War drew to a close. You can read what Sir Arthur Chichester said about the town in Source A.

In 1609 the town and district were granted to Lord Castlehaven, who failed to erect a castle and settle the proper number of English on the land. As a result, these lands reverted to the crown and were then granted to Captain Edmund Leigh and his brothers John and Daniel.

This was not the only place where Lord Castlehaven had not fulfilled his undertaking. Source B is a description of Lord Castlehaven's estate at Forkhill, Co Armagh.

By 1611 the town seems to be well improved. Read Source C.

Later in 1631, Charles I granted the manor of Arleston or Audleston, of 2,000 acres of land in and around Omagh to James Mervyn. Mervyn built three castles. There is now no trace of the castle at Ballynahatty. Of the other two, only the corners remain standing at Trillick and at Kirlish, near Drumquin.

A

Round this place there is great desolation, by reason of which it happeneth that merchants and other passengers weekly guarded travelling from Derrie or Liffer to the Pale are usually in their passage cut off and murdered.

Sir Arthur Chichester's description of Omagh

B

The Earl of Castlehaven hath 3,000 acres. Upon this there is no building at all, either of Bawns or Castle ... I find planted on this land some few English families ... (who) since the old Earl died, (as they tell me) cannot have (land) unless, they will bring treble the rent which they paid; and yet they ... have but half the land which they enjoyed in the old Earl's time ...
The Earl hath more 2,000 acres ... Upon this there was a large house begun, but it is pulled down and made but half so great ... The agent for the Earl showed me the Rent-Roll of all the Tenants ... but they are all leaving the land. The rest of the land is let to 20 Irish Gentlemen ... and these Irish Gentlemen have under them about 3,000 souls of all sorts.

A description of Lord Castlereagh's estate at Forkhill, Co Armagh. From Pynnar's Survey, 1619.

C

The Fort of Omye. Here is a good fort fairly walled with lime and stone about thirty feet high above the ground with a parapet, the river on one side and a large deep ditch about the rest; in which is built a fair house of timber after the English manner. Begun by Captain Edmund Leigh and finished by his brothers, at their own change, upon the lands of the Abbey of Omye, at which place are many families of English and Irish, who have built them good dwelling houses, which is a safety and comfort for passengers between Dungannon and the Liffer. The fort is a place of good import upon all occasions of service and fit to be maintained.

Lord Carew, writing in 1611

D

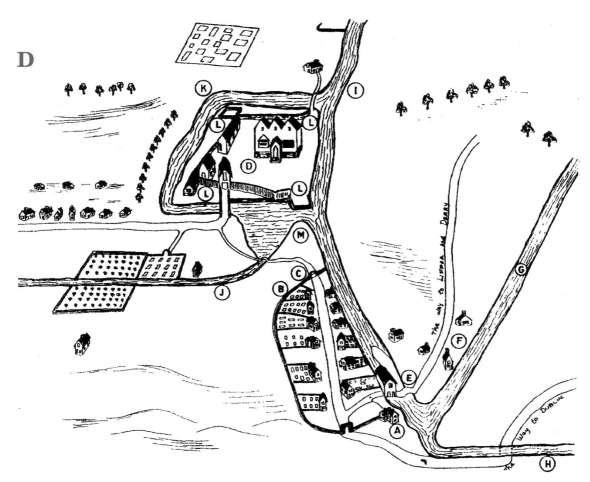

The earliest map of Omagh, 1610

Key

A = Old castle
(Dublin Rd Corner)
B = A cross
C = Northern gate
D = Bawn
E = Mill
F = Inn for Travellers

G = Camowen river
H = Drumragh river
I = Strule river
J = Brook
K = Moat
L = Gun emplacements
M = Gates to the Basin

Questions

1 In what ways is the bawn at Omagh similar to the other examples of bawns which you have seen in Unit 2.6?

2 Who may have drawn the map of Omagh and for what reason?

3 How had Lord Castlehaven failed his undertaking according to Source B?

4 Source A does not give a good impression of the town, so why do you think people were still prepared to take this area from the crown?

5 In what ways has the town and area improved, according to Source C?

2.8 The results of the Ulster Plantation

As expected, the Ulster Plantation changed the country quite dramatically. It did much to make this part of Ireland different from the rest of the country. The rebellious nature of the people was not quashed completely and there was, understandably, opposition to such English intrusion. There were three main results of the plantation: **opposition**, **religious changes**, and the introduction of **a different way of life**.

Opposition

It should not have been unexpected by the colonists that the native Irish would resent their presence. They had been encouraged, from the outset, to provide fortifications and to ensure that their tenants were armed against attack. The main opposition came from the Irish swordsmen who were the armed followers of the dispossessed Irish chiefs. The government had sent some of them into exile but most of them escaped and lived rough in the woods and hills. These people were called **woodkern** (see Source D).

They tried to stop the planters from building and often attacked their farms. This was one of the main reasons why it was so difficult to get English and Scottish tenants to settle on the land.

Religious changes

Many of those who came to Ulster brought with them, from Scotland, their Presbyterian religion. The Presbyterian church permitted ordinary members to play an important part in governing their church. Many of these people would later become very active in Irish revolutionary politics claiming that they should be allowed a part in governing their country as well as their church.

However, not all Scots were regarded as a good influence, as Sources B and C show.

Also, not all planters were Protestant. The Bishop of Derry wrote to the Lord Chancellor in 1629: "Sir George Hamilton ... has done his best to plant Popery ... and has brought over priests ... from Scotland."

A

When the Galloway planters came to Ulster they were only returning to their own lands like emigrants returning home again.

F J Biggar, quoted by I Anderson in *The Identity of Ulster*, Pretani Press, 1982

B

From Scotland came many and from England not a few, yet all of them generally the scum of both nations who from debt or law breaking and fleeing from justice come hither ... most of these people ... cared little for any church ... with fighting, murder, adultery etc.

From *History of the Church of Ireland after the Scots were naturalised*, 1670–71, by Andrew Stewart; edited by WD Killen, Belfast, 1866

C

... the most part were such as either poverty, scandalous lives, or at the best adventurers seeking of better accommodation had forced thither ... the security and thriving of religion was little seen to by these adventurers and the preachers were generally ... the same.

From *The life of Mr Robert Blair*, about 1663, by R Blair; edited by T McCrie, Edinburgh, 1848

Activity

1 Use the library to find out origins of the surnames of the people in your class. Use this information to construct a chart or pie graph showing who has English, Scottish, Irish or other roots.

2 You are a planter from Scotland who has settled in Ulster. Write a letter home to Scotland describing life in your new home. Include details of the settlement, the natives, your church and the difficulties which you are experiencing.

D

B

Woodkern on a raid

Different way of life

These colonists brought to Ulster a way of life so very different from the rest of the country. Many had brought modern farming methods and a tradition of the Puritan work ethic. In Ulster, as a result of the Plantation, both landlord and tenant were usually Protestant and both spoke English. In years to come, these differences would have profound implications for relations between landlord and tenant in Ulster and the rest of the country.

Some Scots had settled in Ulster independently of the plantation scheme. The most important of these were Hugh Montgomery and James Hamilton from Ayrshire. They were very successful, perhaps because they were not regarded as strangers by the Irish.

However, the native Irish were never fully removed from the land and purely British settlements were not established. The rebellion of 1641 shows that the ability of the native Irish in Ulster to wage war was not destroyed by the plantation process, even though it was by then too firmly established to be overthrown.

1 While some people gained much as a result of the Plantation, others were not so pleased. How did (a) Irish Catholics who had lost land, and (b) Irish Protestant landowners who had felt threatened by O'Neill, react to the Plantation?

2 Try to explain why they felt as they did. If possible support your ideas with relevant sources.

Questions

3.1 James I and the Puritans

James was married to Anne of Denmark. They had seven children of whom only three survived childhood.

James believed very strongly in the **Divine Right of Kings**. This meant that he believed absolutely that he had been chosen by God to be King and therefore ordinary people should not question what he said or did.

He disliked the habit of tobacco smoking very much and wrote a pamphlet in 1604 entitled *Counterblasts to Tobacco*, condemning this habit.

James also had many concerns about religion in general. He commissioned an Authorised Version of the Bible in English. This version, sometimes still called the King James Version, came out in 1611.

He was also interested in converting the Psalms into metrical form so that they could be sung. He was doing this himself but died before they were published in 1631.

A

THE
HOLY BIBLE
CONTAINING THE
OLD AND NEW TESTAMENTS
TRANSLATED OUT OF THE ORIGINAL TONGUES: AND WITH THE FORMER TRANSLATIONS DILIGENTLY COMPARED AND REVISED, BY HIS MAJESTY'S SPECIAL COMMAND

APPOINTED TO BE READ IN CHURCHES

B

(One Indian) was their interpreter and was sent from God for their good. He directed them how to set their corn, where to take fish and to gain other types of food and never left them until he died.

William Bradford, leader of the colony

C

Those leaving for Virginia must provide themselves with the following tools for a family of six:
4 hoes, 3 shovels and 2 spades, 2 broad axes,
5 felling axes, 2 steel hand-saws, 2 two-hand saws,
1 whipsaw with file and set 2 augers, 6 chisels,
2 pickaxes, 1 grindstone nails of all sorts.

Advice to pioneers published in England in 1622

The main religious problems in the British Isles at this time

Both James I and Charles I faced opposition from various religious groups. The three main religious groups active at this time are described below.

Anglicans

The Anglican way of worship and the rule of bishops had become common during Elizabeth's reign and the majority of the population wanted this to continue. James himself favoured the Anglicans and this angered the other two religious groups. The leading figure in the Anglican church was **Archbishop Laud** who was bitterly opposed to Puritans.

Puritans

The Puritans were more extreme Protestants who favoured simple church services and a 'religious' lifestyle – the Puritan way of life. As James had been brought up by Puritan nobles in Scotland, the Puritans hoped for favours from the new King. When James I did not favour them, they were angry and a small group left England to found a new state in America. They were known as the **Pilgrim Fathers** and they sailed to America on the *Mayflower* in **1620**. They were intending to go to Virginia but were blown off course and landed hundreds of miles to the north in present day Massachusetts. In the first years friendly Indians helped these settlers. During the next few years thousands of Puritans made their way to the states on the eastern seaboard of America, seeking religious freedom. They also got cheap land and the chance of a fresh start in a new country.

Catholics

The Catholics also hoped for favours from James, and although both his mother and his wife were Catholic, James I ignored their demands once he became King in 1603. As a result, a small number of Catholic nobles began plotting against the King, and this led to the **Gunpowder Plot** of **1605**.

D

The *Mayflower* departing from Plymouth

1. What evidence is there in Source B that this Indian had previous contact with Englishmen?

2. What would the settlers use felling axes for?

3. What is an auger?

4. How can we tell, from Source C, that these settlers would have to build their new homes from scratch?

5. From the point of view of (a) a Puritan and (b) a Roman Catholic, write two letters to James I in 1604, asking him to look favourably on your religion. Mention his background and why, because of this, you think he should favour your cause.

6. Suggest reasons why these letters would differ.

3.2 The Gunpowder Plot

Soon after James became King in 1603 it became clear to leading Catholics in England that they could not expect protection from the new ruler. Therefore they decided to take over the government of England by killing the King and the most important men in the country, when they were together at the state opening of Parliament. Their plan was to blow up Parliament on the 5 November 1605, and put a new Catholic king on the throne.

It now appears very likely that some people close to the King knew of this plot and were prepared to let the plotters go so far as to be found guilty of treason and executed. The plotters rented a cellar beneath the Houses of Parliament without apparently wondering how such good fortune should come their way so easily. It is also a sign of their naïvety that they did not realise just how damp such a cellar would be and the effect this would have on the gunpowder.

James VI of Scotland and I of England

Guy Fawkes and other conspirators in the Gunpowder Plot

There they stored 36 barrels of gunpowder, again with relative ease, never wondering how it could be so easy to do so. They hid the gunpowder under a pile of firewood and laid a trail of it to the door. The plotters assumed it would take about 15 minutes from its ignition until the explosion would take place.

The Monteagle letter

The plot failed because one of the plotters, Francis Tresham, tried to warn his brother-in-law, Lord Monteagle, to stay away from the state opening of Parliament. Tresham sent a very mysterious letter to Monteagle and it was shown to James I. The letter raised the King's suspicions and he ordered a search of the cellars of the House of Lords on the 4 November. This led to the arrest of **Guy Fawkes** and after being tortured in the Tower of London, he confessed his role in the Gunpowder Plot.

Lord Monteagle's family was Catholic and he had been involved in a rebellion in 1601 against Queen Elizabeth I. He was released from prison after paying a heavy fine. In 1603 he supported King James, and in 1605 he wrote to the King saying he had become a Protestant (see Source D). Lord Monteagle was even allowed to sit in the House of Lords.

Guy Fawkes
in a cellar under
the Houses of Parliament

C

My lord – out of the love I bear to some of your friends, I have a care of your preservation. Therefore I warn you ... to devise some excuse to shift your attendance at this Parliament ... They shall receive a terrible blow this Parliament and yet they shall not see who hurts them ... The danger is past as soon as you have burnt this letter.

An extract from the Monteagle letter

D

I will live and die in that religion which I have now resolved to profess.

Lord Monteagle in 1605

Activity

Write a newspaper report following the discovery of the Gunpowder Plot.

Questions

1 **Why do you think Tresham sent the letter (Source C) to Monteagle?**

2 **How might Monteagle's comments about his religion (Source D) have influenced his decision to show the letter to the King?**

3.3   Charles I and Parliament

Charles I

Born in 1600, second son of James VI of Scotland and Queen Anne. His elder brother Henry died in 1612.

- a sickly child, bandy-legged and had a stutter
- very deeply religious especially favouring Roman Catholicism
- loved painting especially Italian and Belgian art
- married a French princess, Henrietta Maria, with whom he had seven children
- believed he had been sent by God to govern and had to answer only to God for his actions.

Cromwell

Born in 1599 in Huntingdon, and it is said that as a boy (in 1604) he fought the young Prince Charles when the latter was staying at Cromwell's grandfather's home. The boys quarrelled over a toy and Cromwell made the Prince's nose bleed!

- became the greatest Civil War commander
- a very strict Puritan.

There were two main reasons why Parliament defied the King:

1 **Religion** – Charles was very sympathetic to the Roman Catholics and his wife was a Catholic. He may have wished to ally England with Spain. Most members of Parliament were Protestant and many of these were strict Puritans.

2 **Parliament wanted more power** – members of Parliament wanted regular elections and they resented the King raising taxes or making new laws without the consent of Parliament.

The King had quarrelled so much with Parliament that in 1629 he dismissed it and ruled for 11 years on his own. This did not make him popular. In 1640 he had to recall Parliament as he was so short of money. During the next year Parliament consistently tried to limit the King's power. Charles was so angry about this that, in January 1642, he marched into the House of Commons to arrest the five MPs who had most annoyed him. They had escaped and this action usually marked the beginning of the English Civil War. (He was the last monarch to enter the House of Commons.)

In this Civil War, like others, it is difficult to define clearly who supported each side. One village may have supported the King, while its neighbour was on Parliament's side. Indeed some families were divided over this issue also. The boxes on the next page give some idea who supported each side.

A dramatic painting of the Battle of Marston Moor, 1644 – one of the decisive battles of the Civil War

Groups of people who supported Parliament in the Civil War

Scots
Navy
Farmers
Townsfolk
Merchants
Roundheads

Groups of people who supported the King in the Civil War

Noblemen
Servants of noblemen
Welsh
Cavaliers

Activity

Divide your page into two columns. List the groups which supported Parliament on one side and those which supported the King on the other. In each case, suggest why they were on one side or the other.

Questions

Explain what were the main causes of the argument between King and Parliament.

3.4 The English Civil War

1642	22 August	War declared.
	23 October	Battle of Edgehill – Royalist victory.
	13 Nov	King retreats to HQ in Oxford.
1643	Jan–May	Royalists do well in North, East, Midlands, Wales and Borders & West.
		Parliament does well in South and Central England.
	20 Sept	Inconclusive first battle of Newbury.
	25 Sept	20,000 Scottish troops come to help Parliament.
1644	19 January	Scottish army enters England.
	Jan–March	Royalist defeats in N Midlands and South.
	2 July	Cromwell wins at Marston Moor.
	27 October	Inconclusive second battle of Newbury.
1645	February	Unsuccessful peace negotiations.
	April	New Model Army created.
	14 June	Battle of Naseby.
	June–Sept	New Model Army has several victories.
1646	5 May	King surrenders to Scots and is taken to Newcastle.
	13 July	Peace terms presented to the King.
1647	March	Scottish army goes home.
	May	Short of money, Parliament pays off most of the New Model Army.
	June	Army refuses to retire until properly paid and a fair settlement reached with the King.
	1 August	Army puts forward its own peace terms.
	26 Dec	King persuades Scots to join his side and invade England.
1648	March–May	Royalists defeated by New Model Army in South East and Wales.
	2 August	Scots defeated at Preston.
	6 Dec	Army officers take over Parliament.
1649	20 January	This new Parliament puts the King on trial.
	27 January	Death sentence declared on the King.
	30 January	Charles I executed.
	February	House of Lords and Monarchy abolished.

A

A Cavalier, who supported the King

Activity

In groups, compose speeches to be delivered to their respective armies by the King and by Oliver Cromwell.
Explain in these why you are fighting and why victory is essential to your side.

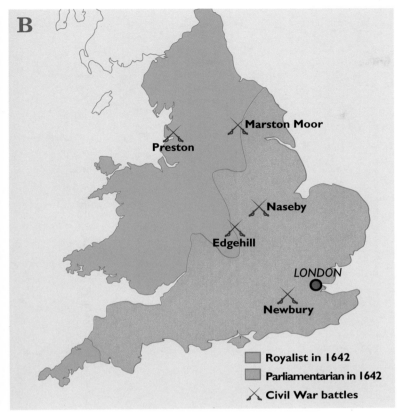

Main battles in the English Civil War

A Roundhead, who supported
Parliament

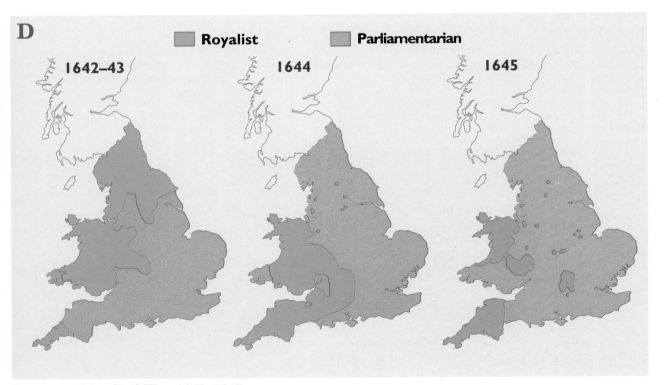

Progress of the Civil War, 1642–1645

When the Civil War began in 1642 the King's supporters (Cavaliers) and Parliament's supporters (Roundheads) were evenly matched.

From the outset, however, the King appeared to have an advantage, because the nobles who supported him were skilled horsemen, but this was more than wiped out by the formation of the **New Model Army**. This new army quickly proved itself to be a very professional and efficient force which would guarantee Parliament's success in the Civil War.

In 1646 the King surrendered, and the New Model Army offered to let Charles remain King if he would agree to let everyone except Catholics worship as they pleased. The King was a proud man and as he did not want either Parliament or the army to dictate terms to him, he began plotting against Parliament. This resulted in the re-opening of the Civil War in 1648, but again Charles was decisively beaten. Naturally, the army generals were furious at the King's attempts to deceive them, and although many MPs in Parliament urged caution, the army was determined to execute Charles.

Execution of Charles I at Whitehall, 1649

Activity

Use the information in Units 3.3, 3.4 and 3.5 to write Charles I's obituary.

The nature of the war

◆ Both armies were very similar; each regiment had ten companies, a total of 1,200 men.

◆ Each company had its own flag. Companies had musketeers and pikemen – usually twice as many musketeers as pikemen. Much of the fighting was done by musketeers, many of whom blew themselves up loading the muskets. Pikemen fought other pikemen and defended musketeers.

◆ The cavalry was organised in regiments and usually fought on the flanks of the army with the infantry in the centre.

◆ Many sieges also took place. From April 1645 to August 1646, the New Model Army took part in 11 field battles and 50 sieges.

Charles I's execution

In January 1649 the House of Commons set up a court to try the King. Part of the charge against him read:

regicide – the killing of a monarch

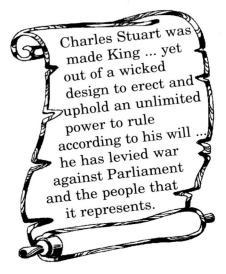

Charles Stuart was made King ... yet out of a wicked design to erect and uphold an unlimited power to rule according to his will ... he has levied war against Parliament and the people that it represents.

1 What did Charles mean by his final words?

2 Do you think Oliver Cromwell would have agreed with him?

3 Why do you think only 59 judges signed the death warrant?

4 What sort of accidents could take place in battle?

5 What can you tell from the figures about the deaths caused by war?

Charles was asked to reply to this charge but all he said was that he did not accept that the court had any right to put him on trial. However, Charles was still declared guilty and sentenced to death on 27 January 1649. Only 59 of the 135 judges signed his death warrant. His execution took place three days later. It is said that he asked for an extra vest so that he would not shiver with cold and people think it was fear. On the scaffold he again claimed his innocence. His final words were "I go from a corruptible to an uncorruptible crown, where no disturbance can be, no disturbance in the world".

The cost of the war

It is thought that 17% of Parliamentarians and 12% of Royalists died in the nine major battles. At this time, the population was just over five million, of which 1.5 million were adult males.

Disease also killed many. Plagues of typhoid and diarrhoea spread in many areas.

Casualty figures

	Killed	Prisoner
Parliament	34,141	34,493
Royalist	50,579	83,041
Total	84,738	117,534

Direct deaths from combat	84,738
Deaths from disease	100,000
Accidents	300
Total	185,038

3.5   Oliver Cromwell

During the Civil War **Oliver Cromwell** (Source A) emerged as the leading figure on the side of Parliament. He had become an MP in 1640, and by 1646 he was a very successful general and the idol of the army. He also had great political gifts. Therefore, he was an ideal link between the army and Parliament. It was his position in the army, however, that enabled Cromwell to increase his own power, as the generals, rather than Parliament, were actually in charge of the country. By the early 1650s Cromwell was clearly the most powerful man in the country, and in 1653 he was given a new title, the **Lord Protector of the Commonwealth of England**, a position he held until his death in 1658.

Cromwell's influence

Cromwell was a deeply religious man and tried to instill Puritan values on everyday life in England.

As a general he believed that he was fighting God's battles, while in politics he was convinced that every decision he made had to reflect God's will. There is no doubt that his sincere religious beliefs influenced his actions in Ireland in 1649–1650.

Cromwell is one of the most important figures in the history of the British Isles. Yet unlike many of the other great figures in history he is remembered with little affection. The cruelty associated with his rule has influenced the way in which people think about him, but there is no doubt that Cromwell changed the course of English history. Parliament became more important, and the process by which power was transferred from the monarch to the people could not be stopped. One other consequence of Cromwell's rule was that future English governments were always careful to ensure that the army would never again become involved in politics.

Oliver Cromwell

The effect of Cromwell's rule in England and Wales

England no longer had a king, and the House of Lords was abolished. In the Church, Bishops were abolished and each individual church was run by the minister and a committee elected by the congregation. Nearly all previous forms of entertainment (dancing, fairs, etc) were banned. Most of the people did not enjoy the strict conditions imposed by Puritan rule. Catholics were prosecuted if they tried to practise their religion.

The effect of Cromwell's rule in Scotland

The Scots were angered by Charles I's execution and they crowned his son, Prince Charles, as their King.

He then led an army into England in an attempt to regain the throne but was defeated by Cromwell.

disinter – dig up

After Cromwell's death his supporters quarrelled among themselves and were unable to govern the country firmly. By 1660 they decided to bring back the king. **Charles II**, the son of Charles I, agreed to rule on conditions which his father had always rejected, and he became King in May **1660**. The return of the King is called **The Restoration**.

After the Restoration in 1660, Cromwell's body was disinterred and exposed to derision on the gallows of Tyburn.

There have been many different judgements made about Cromwell. You can read some of them in Source B.

B

... a brave, bad man
(Earl of Clarendon, mid-17th century)

... a bulldozer who has wrecked civil life
(Andrew Maxwell, 1650)

... he inspired no fondness but profound mistrust even – perhaps especially – among men nearest him ... all complained at his slipperness
(Blair Worden, a 20th century historian)

C

... wonderful works of God, breaking the rod of the oppressor, as in the day of Midian

Words used by Cromwell after his victories

Questions

1 Which groups of people in England and Scotland would have disliked the rules made by Cromwell about (a) religion and (b) entertainment?

2 What reasons do you think Cromwell would have given for making these changes?

3 Select words or items from Source B which are (a) favourable and (b) unfavourable about Cromwell.

4 How do the words used by Cromwell (Source C) confirm the view which he held that he was only doing God's work?

5 Why do you think Cromwell never accepted the title of King even though he had the power?

3.6 Cromwell's campaign in Ireland

To understand why Cromwell came to Ireland we must look back to the **Ulster Rebellion** of **1641**. This rebellion can be viewed in two ways:

(a) The Ulster Catholics who had been forced to surrender their lands to English and Scottish planters were striking back at the new Protestant settlers.

(b) It became part of the Civil War as the Catholics in Ireland took the side of the King in his struggle against Parliament.

The Ulster Rebellion resulted in the deaths of 10,000 to 15,000 Protestants, some of whom were massacred in particularly cruel incidents, such as at the River Bann near Portadown.

The stories of these massacres were greatly exaggerated and by the time the Puritans in the House of Commons were informed about these events, estimates of up to 300,000 Protestants being slaughtered were commonly believed in England. Parliament was determined that this rebellion should be crushed and it was decided that the cost of this exercise should be paid for by confiscating Irish land.

The Civil War in England meant that only a small force could be sent to Ireland in **1642** and the result was military stalemate for the next seven years. This was to change in **1649** however, when following the King's execution, it was decided to send an army to Ireland to crush the enemies of the Commonwealth.

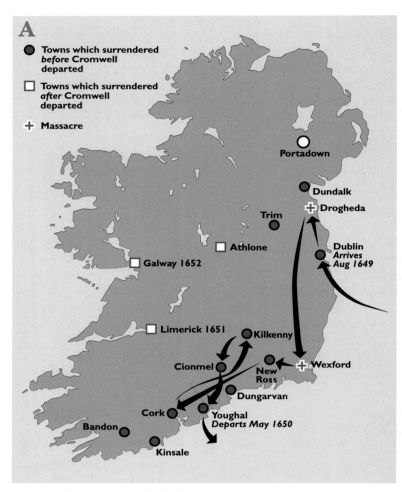

A

● Towns which surrendered *before* Cromwell departed

□ Towns which surrendered *after* Cromwell departed

✚ Massacre

Portadown

Dundalk

✚ Drogheda

Trim

Athlone

Dublin *Arrives Aug 1649*

Galway 1652

Limerick 1651

Kilkenny

Cionmel

New Ross

✚ Wexford

Dungarvan

Cork

Youghal *Departs May 1650*

Bandon

Kinsale

Cromwell's campaign in Ireland

Questions

1 Do you regard Source C as a reliable account of the events of 1649? Explain your answer.

2 Using the information in this unit, say what it was like to live in Ireland in the 1640s.

3 What other evidence would you need to have to find out what life in the 1640s was really like?

B

[In 1649] Oliver Cromwell was sent to Ireland to deal with the Catholic rebellion. The methods he used to crush the rebels were harsh. When English soldiers captured the garrison of the town of Drogheda they ran wild, killing nearly 3000 people (including 200 women).

From *The Irish Question* by Hamish Macdonald, 1985

Look at the statements below and say whether you believe them to be true or false. Give evidence from the sources to support your ideas.

1 In 1649 all the Catholics in Drogheda were killed by Cromwell.

2 Women, the old and children were all attacked in Drogheda.

Cromwell himself took charge of the army (12,000 men), and it landed at **Ringsend** near Dublin in **August 1649**. One of the first objectives for Cromwell's army was the town of **Drogheda**. It was occupied by a small force (a garrison), and after a very brief siege the town was stormed by Cromwell's troops in September 1649 after the walls had been breached by cannon fire. Most of the defending soldiers and many of the town's inhabitants were killed in this attack.

News of this slaughter spread quickly with the result that neighbouring Catholic towns surrendered to avoid a repeat of the events in Drogheda.

Cromwell's actions in Drogheda have been fiercely criticised by subsequent generations of Irishmen. He himself saw the massacre as fair punishment for the murder of Protestants in 1641; indeed he judged the entire episode as a "righteous judgement of God upon these barbarous wretches".

After Drogheda Cromwell marched his troops south, and a similar attack took place on Wexford with many of the Catholic population being massacred. For Cromwell this had the desired effect as the neighbouring towns of New Ross, Cork, Bandon, Kinsale and Youghal quickly surrendered, once news of the events in Wexford reached them. Other towns surrendered in the spring of 1650 and although some fighting continued for a further two years, Cromwell was able to leave Ireland in 1650 in the knowledge that he had obtained a crushing victory over the Catholic rebels.

C

When the city was captured by the heretics, the blood of the Catholics was mercilessly shed in the streets, in the dwelling houses and in the open fields. To none was mercy shown; not to women, nor to the aged, nor to the young. The majority of the citizens became the prey of the parliamentary troops.

A Jesuit priest's eyewitness account of the attack on Drogheda

stalemate – when neither side in a conflict can win

breached – broken through

3.7 The Cromwellian Settlement

As well as taking revenge against the Irish Catholics for the rebellion they began in 1641, Cromwell knew he had an economic reason for having to conquer Ireland. The government in London needed money to repay loans which had been made during the English Civil War, and many officers in the New Model Army were owed huge amounts of back-pay. In place of money which the government did not have, Cromwell had already decided to pay these men with grants of land – land which was seized from the Catholic rebels after their defeat.

In fact, Cromwell's control of Ireland was guaranteed when nearly 35,000 Catholic soldiers left Ireland to join the armies of Catholic France and Spain. The English government hoped that its control over Ireland could be extended by a new scheme of plantation similar to the Ulster Plantation, but the attempt to attract large numbers of Protestant settlers to Ireland was a failure.

This meant that ordinary Catholics stayed in their homes, but their rents were paid to the new Protestant landowners. A number of Catholic landowners were allowed to keep some property, but they still had to leave their traditional lands and take instead much smaller and poorer holdings in the west. County Clare and most of the counties in Connaught were reserved for these Catholic landowners and their families. The west had, of course, the poorest farming land in Ireland, and the Catholics who were sent there were not allowed to live in towns or within three miles of the coast, as all coastal land was given to Cromwellian soldiers.

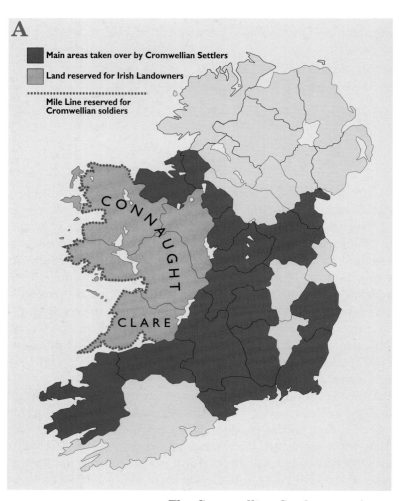

A

■ Main areas taken over by Cromwellian Settlers

■ Land reserved for Irish Landowners

•••••••• Mile Line reserved for Cromwellian soldiers

CONNAUGHT

CLARE

The Cromwellian Settlement of 1652

B

I meddle not with any man's conscience, but if by liberty of conscience you mean a liberty to exercise the Mass, I judge it best to use plain dealing, and let you know where the Parliament of England have power, that will not be allowed.

Cromwell's comments on the Catholic religion in Ireland

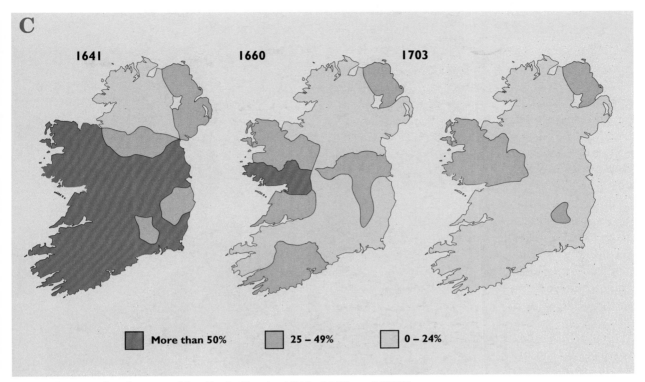

C

1641   1660   1703

More than 50%   25 – 49%   0 – 24%

Maps showing lands owned by Catholics in 1641, 1660 and 1703

The end result of the **Cromwellian Settlement 1652** was the transfer of wealth and power to Protestants who now owned most of the land.

Not surprisingly, Cromwell's government in England, which was dominated by Puritans, did its utmost to make life very difficult for Catholics. Many were executed, while others were imprisoned or forced to leave the country. Indeed most of the Catholic clergy, numbering about 1,000 priests, were forced out of Ireland in the 1650s. When Charles II became King in 1660, he made very few changes to the Cromwellian land settlement, but he did relax the persecution against the Catholic Church in Ireland.

persecution – ill-treatment

Questions

1 Look at Source A. Why do you think Catholics were not allowed to live on the coast?

2 According to Source A, three areas – Ulster, Munster and south of Dublin– do not appear to be part of this settlement. Can you suggest any reasons for this?

3 Look at Source C. In which areas did Catholics continue to hold at least 25% of the land between 1641 and 1703?

4 Suggest why they lost land in other areas.

5 Did Catholics lose more land in the period 1641–1660 or in the period 1660–1703? Explain your conclusion.

4.1 Europe in 1688

In 1688 war broke out in Europe between the French King, **Louis XIV**, and a league of European states, known as the **Grand Alliance**. This war lasted until 1697.

This Grand Alliance was led by **William of Orange** and consisted of the Spanish King whose Empire included the Spanish Netherlands; the Holy Roman Emperor who ruled the German states; and the rulers of Prussia and Bavaria (see Source A).

Some kings and rulers who were not members of the Grand Alliance wanted Louis defeated so that Europe could be at peace. **James II** of England did not join the alliance in 1688 as he felt that England was in no danger at that time. Besides, he wanted to remain on good terms with the Dutch and the French.

James had become King of England in 1685 and, even though he was a Catholic, no one really objected to him. However, there was one small rebellion led by the Duke of Monmouth. After this, James kept a large army and also promoted many Catholics to officer status. He tried to introduce forms of religious tolerance for non-Anglicans (people who were not members of the Church of England).

Parliament became increasingly suspicious of him and feared that he was trying to make England a Catholic country. There was also concern that he might persecute Protestants as Louis XIV was doing in France. James's heir to the throne was his elder daughter, **Mary**, who was married to William of Orange.

A

- Members of Grand Alliance 1689
- France and her Allies
- Ottoman Empire
- Boundary of Holy Roman Empire

Europe in 1688

Louis XIV

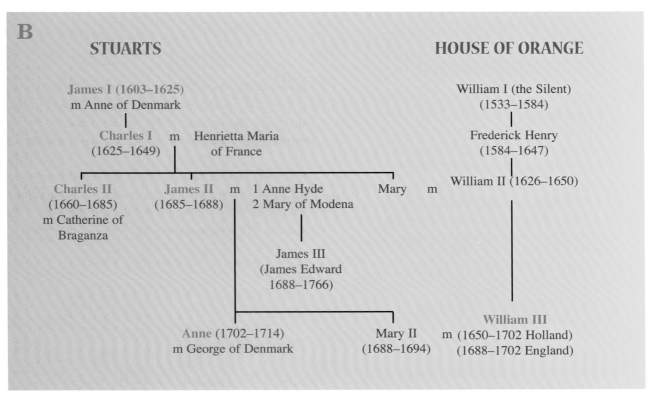

| STUARTS | | | | | HOUSE OF ORANGE |

B

STUARTS

HOUSE OF ORANGE

James I (1603–1625)
m Anne of Denmark

William I (the Silent)
(1533–1584)

Charles I   m   Henrietta Maria
(1625–1649)   of France

Frederick Henry
(1584–1647)

Charles II   James II   m   1 Anne Hyde   Mary   m   William II (1626–1650)
(1660–1685)   (1685–1688)   2 Mary of Modena
m Catherine of
Braganza

James III
(James Edward
1688–1766)

Anne (1702–1714)   Mary II   William III
m George of Denmark   (1688–1694)   m (1650–1702 Holland)
                                                   (1688–1702 England)

The Stuart and Orange family trees

In June 1688, however, James's second wife **Mary of Modena** had a son. This changed things dramatically. The boy – who was a Catholic – would succeed his father, displacing his two older Protestant sisters, Mary and Anne. To prevent a Catholic becoming king, the English Parliament invited William of Orange, Mary's husband, to take the English throne.

Mary II, wife of William and daughter of James II

William landed on the south coast of England in November 1688 and moved to London. James II, with his wife and son, fled to France. William and Mary were made joint monarchs in February 1689. This is known as the **Glorious Revolution**. William had been eager to come to England, because he hoped to add English support to his struggle against Louis XIV. However, he soon found that his attention was diverted to events in Ireland.

Activity

Write a letter from Mary to her sister Anne, in November 1688, explaining her position as daughter of the deposed King and the wife of the new one.

Questions

Using the information in this unit, explain the reasons why Parliament believed that William had the best claim to the English throne in 1688.

67

4.2 James II and Ireland

A

December 1688: Frequently, before the siege actually commenced, we had been alarmed by reports that the Roman Catholics intended to rise in arms against us and to act over the tragedy of 1641 ... At last a regiment of them raised by the Marquis of Antrim, actually arrived at Newtownlimavady, on their march to Derry ... These set us immediately to consider what was to be done; but we could not determine among ourselves what was best.

While we were in this confused hesitation, on the 7 December 1688, a few resolute apprentice boys determined for us. These ran to the Gates and shut them, drew up the bridge, and seized the magazine. This, like magic, roused an unanimous spirit of defence and now with one voice we determined to maintain the city at all hazards, and each sex and age joined in the important cause.

Thomas Ash, a Protestant from Co Londonderry

Ireland was still ruled by England in the late seventeenth century and the land was divided among the various settlers and the native Catholic population. The result of the Cromwellian Settlement (1652) was to divide Irish society into landowners on one side and a great number of small tenant-farmers, called cottiers, on the other.

During James's reign much had been done to improve the position for Catholics just as had happened in England. Many former landowners also hoped that James would restore their estates to them. In **1687** James had made his brother-in-law, **Richard Talbot**, the King's representative in Ireland. His official title was **Lord Lieutenant**, but he was also known as the **Earl of Tyrconnell**, or even as 'Lying Dick'. He strengthened the Irish army in case it was needed to support James.

In 1688 Tyrconnell sent troops to Ulster, but the garrisons in Derry and Enniskillen would not admit them. Protestants in Ireland declared their support for William and Mary and prepared to fight for them. Those who supported William are usually call **Williamites**, while James's supporters are known as **Jacobites**. A leading Ulster Jacobite was the **Earl of Antrim**.

B

December 1688: The first of Ireland's Protestants who appeared for the Prince of Orange were the inhabitants of Londonderry.

The burgesses hearing thereof, and that the king was abandoned by his army and by the people of England, did resolutely, about the beginning of December 1688, shut up their gates against the said regiment ... About the same time the viceroy sent two companies to be quartered at Enniskillen, a small inland town in the same province. This also refused entrance to the king's garrison.

Nicholas Plunkett, a contemporary Jacobite author and supporter of Tyrconnell

C

Finding the people of Londonderry continue obstinate to their rebellion, and that there appears no likelihood of reducing them by fair means. I desire your lordship to give orders presently, to all the companies of your regiment, to be in readiness to march at an hours warning, it being my resolution in case I doe not hear, by fridays post, that the City of Derry has submitted, to order them, with several other regiments of horse, foot and dragoons, to march against it, and will soon follow them myself. I am, My lord yr ldps most faythfull humble servant.

Tyrconnell

A letter from Earl of Tyrconnell to the Earl of Antrim, 1688

James VII and II, by Sir Peter Lely
(He was James VII of Scotland and II of England.)

unanimous –
supported by everyone
concerned

1 Sources A, B and C are all primary evidence. How useful are they to an historian?

2 Which sentences in Source A show a change in the attitude of the people of Derry?

3 How does Source B differ from Source A in its description of the closure of the gates? Suggest a reason for this difference.

4 Do the differences between Sources A and B mean that they are unreliable? Explain your answer.

5 Why do you think the word 'rebellion' was used in Source C to describe events in Derry?

4.3   The Williamite Wars

James arrived in Ireland from France in March 1689, landing at Kinsale and arriving in Dublin on 24 March. By that time many groups of Protestants throughout Ulster were fighting back. When they were unsuccessful, many fled to England or Scotland, while some took refuge in fortified towns such as Derry.

This quarrel which was emerging between William and James was part of the on-going war in Europe between the French King, Louis XIV, and the Grand Alliance, led by William. In fact, the Pope was against the French King and had special prayers of thanksgiving said in Rome when news reached him that William had defeated James, who was supported by the French. Because of Louis XIV's involvement, this war in Ireland became known as the **War of the Three Kings** and lasted from 1688 to 1691.

On James II's side, the main army leaders were his brother-in-law, the **Earl of Tyrconnell** and **Patrick Sarsfield** who was the defender of Limerick. James' supporters were called **Jacobites** and they consisted of 25,000 men of whom 6,000 were French who had been in battle before. The rest were inexperienced. He had no cannon and just twelve French field pieces. The soldiers had scythes or sharpened sticks.

William's supporters, known as **Williamites**, were larger in number and better equipped. He had 36,000 men including Blue Dutch Guards, Danes, German Branden-burgers and French Protestants. These soldiers were well trained mercenaries. They had good artillery with 50 to 60 large cannon and several mortars. They also had up to date flintlock muskets and bayonets. Two major army leaders were **Ginkel**, who became First Earl of Athlone and fought at the Battle of Aughrim, and **Schomberg** who was killed at the Boyne.

The Jacobite leader, Patrick Sarsfield

The Williamite commander, General Ginkel

A

William III

GUILELMUS. III.
D.G. ANGLIÆ, SCOTIÆ, FRANCIÆ
ET. HYBERNIÆ, REX.

D   Colours worn by

Jacobites	Williamites
white, yellow, blue, red with orange lining, red with white lining, white lined with red.	blue, white, buff coats/coloured sashes, red with yellow facings, blue with yellow facings, green with white facings.

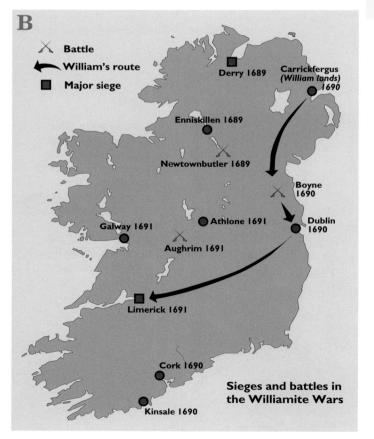

B

✗ Battle

← William's route

■ Major siege

Derry 1689

Carrickfergus
(William lands)
1690

Enniskillen 1689

Newtownbutler 1689

Boyne
1690

Galway 1691

Athlone 1691

Dublin
1690

Aughrim 1691

Limerick 1691

Cork 1690

Kinsale 1690

**Sieges and battles in
the Williamite Wars**

1 **What is a mercenary?**

2 **What are the advantages
   and disadvantages of having
   mercenaries on your side in a
   battle?**

3 **Name two problems which may
   occur in an army consisting of
   various nationalities.**

4 **How do Sources C & D show that
   confusion could take place on the
   battlefield?**

5 **Using the information given
   about the leaders and the relative
   strengths of the forces, which side
   do you think had the best chance
   of winning? Give reasons for your
   answers.**

4.4　The Siege of Derry

In the last unit we read how the apprentice boys of Derry had shut the gates against the advancing Jacobite army in December 1688. To some people in the city of Derry this was seen as treason against their lawful King, James. For others, this action was vital for their security.

When James arrived in Ireland in **March 1689**, he was determined to crush all remaining opposition. One of his first actions was to demand the surrender of Derry, the Williamite stronghold which was then under the command of **Colonel Lundy**. This marked the beginning of the siege which would last 105 days. Governor Lundy and the city council considered surrendering. He was discredited for this and forced to leave. The **Rev George Walker** became the new Governor of the city. On **4 June 1689** a boom was placed across the Foyle leaving those defending the city cut off and running very short of supplies.

The Jacobites were short of heavy artillery, but they increased the weight of shot fired.

A

Our drink was nothing but water, which we paid very dear for, and could not get without danger.

George Walker, Governor of Derry

B

Everyday some ... deserted the garrison, so that the enemy received constant intelligence of our proceedings. This gave some trouble and made us remove our ammunition very often ... Our iron ball is now all spent, and instead of them we make balls of brick, cast over with lead, to the weight and size of our iron-ball.

George Walker, Governor of Derry

C

Activity

Form groups. You are reporters for a 1689 version of the main evening news. Construct a report from the City of Derry, describing living conditions there and the difficulties experienced by the besieging Jacobite forces.

An artist's impression of the apprentice boys closing the city gates during the Siege of Derry, 1689

D

Date	Big	Small
April 24 – 27	0	17
April 27 – 6 May	0	6
June 2 – 21 July	261	326
July 22	0	42
July 23	0	20

Cannon shot or mortar bombs used against the City of Derry in 1689

E

... the cold which the men – specially the women and children contracted, hereby, added to their want of rest and food, occasioned diseases in the garrison, as fevers, flux, etc of which great numbers died.

John Mackenzie (Presbyterian chaplain to Walker's Regiment)

F

Horse flesh sold for 1s 8d per pound	
A quarter of a dog	5s 6d
A dog's head	2s 6d
A cat	4s 6d
A pound of tallow	4s 0d
A pound of salted Hides	1s 0d
A quarter of Horse Blood	1s 0d
A rat	1s 0d
A mouse	0s 6d
A horse pudding	0s 6d
A handful of chick weed	0s 1d
A quart of meal when found	1s 0d

Prices of food during the Siege of Derry.
1s means one shilling and equals 5p. 6d means 6 pennies and was half of one shilling.

Conditions in the city deteriorated. Look at Sources A, B, D, E and F and you will see that the defenders were short of ammunition, food and supplies. They were also subjected to many diseases (Source E).

A relief force arrived in Lough Foyle on 13 June but did not try to break through the boom. The ship's captain claimed that when he had not heard from the city's defenders, he assumed they did not need his help. Eventually on **28 July** the ship's captain, Major-General Kirke, was told by London to break the boom. The ship, called *The Mountjoy*, broke the boom, ending the siege. The soldiers who had followed James left as quickly as possible. Both armies suffered heavy casualties.

While the siege was taking place in Derry, the garrison at **Enniskillen** intercepted the Jacobites at Newtownbutler and forced them to divide their forces, keeping half the Jacobite army from going to Derry.

In August **Schomberg** landed at Carrickfergus, captured it after a brief siege, and soon all of Ulster was in Williamite hands.

Questions

1 List the problems experienced by those inside the city during the siege.

2 Explain why you think the citizens of Derry were prepared to put up with these conditions.

4.5 The Battle of the Boyne

A

Seventeenth-century siege guns in use: firing, cooling the barrel, cooling the breech with sheepskins soaked in water

B

The day was very clear, as if the Sun itself had a mind to see what would happen.

George Story, a chaplain in Schomberg's army

At the beginning of March 1690 four thousand Danes arrived in Belfast to help William. Within a week more reinforcements had arrived from England. Many of the Danes were keen to end the war in Ireland and bring William back to take charge once again of the Grand Alliance in the European conflict. At the same time Louis XIV agreed to send James some battle-hardened French soldiers. Louis wanted the war to continue in Ireland so that William would be kept out of the European conflict.

In June 1690 **William** arrived at **Carrickfergus** and marched on Dundalk. King James moved north from Dublin to meet him. On **1 July 1690** the two armies met at the **River Boyne** in Co Meath.

The calendar was 11 days out so when it was adjusted, the date of the battle was changed to 12 July 1690.

Activity

1 Use the library and any other books available to find pictures of William and James at the Boyne. Suggest why many differences appear in these pictures.

2 Using the map and the information about troops from pages 70 and 71, devise the orders for battle which may have been issued by the Commanding Officer on each side to his army. Instruct them on the best tactics to use, where to position the different sections of their men, bearing in mind the land around them, their armaments and the skill of the soldiers.

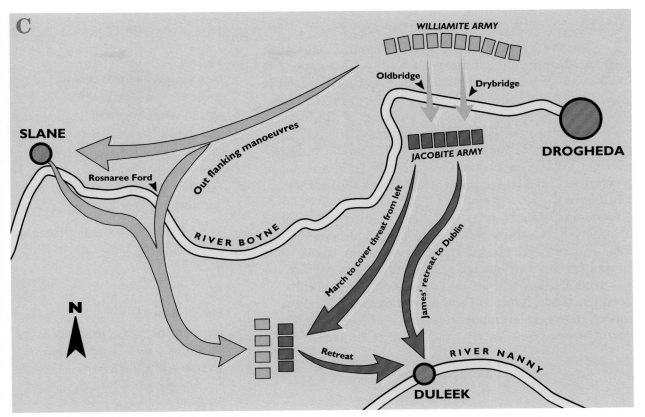

C

WILLIAMITE ARMY

Oldbridge   Drybridge

SLANE

Rosnaree Ford

Out flanking manoeuvres

JACOBITE ARMY   DROGHEDA

RIVER BOYNE

March to cover threat from left

James' retreat to Dublin

N

Retreat   RIVER NANNY

DULEEK

The Battle of the Boyne, 1 July 1690

James believed that William's main attack would come from Rosnaree so he moved more than half of his army in that direction. However, at that point the ground was marshy and no fighting was to take place there.

Instead the Williamite army crossed between Oldbridge and Drybridge. The Duke of Schomberg and the Rev George Walker were killed there.

Although the Jacobites were heavily outnumbered the battle lasted for two hours. William's army crossed the river first and the Jacobite cavalry fought well. When James saw that the battle was lost, he fled with his bodyguard to Dublin, before setting sail for France. The Jacobite losses numbered about 1,300, while the Williamites lost about 400.

Because William was part of the European Grand Alliance, there was rejoicing throughout Europe that he had defeated an ally of Louis XIV.

Questions

1 List the reasons why William was victorious at the Boyne.

2 Which reason do you think was the most important and why?

3 What further evidence is there in this unit that this battle was part of the European conflict?

4 How can we tell that James' forces were not easy to defeat?

After he had lost at the Boyne, James is reported to have been told, "Don't worry about it; in two weeks nobody will remember a thing about it!"

4.6 Limerick and Aughrim

After the Battle of the Boyne, Tyrconnell was prepared to negotiate with William. However, some other Jacobites such as Sarsfield refused to do so. They hoped for better peace terms from William if they could hold out for longer. The rest of the Irish army was concentrated in Limerick and Athlone. Early in August 1690 William laid siege to Limerick. Patrick Sarsfield led the defenders in Limerick. He managed to intercept and destroy a great quantity of William's guns at Ballineedy.

Although William was still able to launch an attack on Limerick, the Jacobites were able to hold out.

As autumn and the heavy rains set in, William finally gave up and left Ireland. He left General Ginkel in charge. Ginkel offered peace to Sarsfield and the Jacobites. They rejected this, however, and decided to fight on. Ginkel then prepared for a final assault. The Jacobites were now led by the **Marquis St Ruth**.

A

William, having made a larger breach in the wall, gave a general assault which lasted for three hours; and though his men mounted the breach, and some even entered the town, they were gallantly repulsed and forced to retire with considerable loss.

Charles O'Kelly, a Gaelic Irishman, speaking about the siege at Limerick

B

The Irish ventured upon the breach again, and from the walls and every place so pester'd us upon the counterscarp, that after nigh three hours resisting bullets, stones, broken bottles ... and whatever way could be thought on to destroy us, our ammunition being spent, it was judged safest to return to our trenches.

George Story, a Williamite

1 In what ways do the accounts in Source A and B of the last days of the siege differ?

2 How do you account for these differences?

3 "Any historical source is useful to a historian." Do you agree? Refer to the sources and the map in this unit in your answer.

4 Why do you think the Williamites won at Aughrim?

5 What does William's departure from Ireland indicate about his commitment to the war there?

A modern Orange banner showing King William crossing the Boyne

By the summer of 1691 the Jacobites were at Aughrim blocking Ginkel's approach to Galway. Sarsfield suggested that the Jacobite army withdraw to Limerick, but St Ruth had the stronger position in higher ground, while the Williamites would have to cross a bog. However, the Williamites had twice as many heavy guns and Ginkel gave the order to attack, even though his men had just completed a long march.

St Ruth was killed in battle and this left the Jacobites in disarray. Most of their forces retreated to Limerick. Ginkel followed them there and it seemed as though there would be another long siege. However, the failure of French help to arrive and the sudden death of Tyrconnell persuaded other Jacobite leaders to agree to Ginkel's peace terms. Consequently, the Jacobites surrendered on 26 September 1691 and a treaty was signed in October 1691.

repulsed – driven back

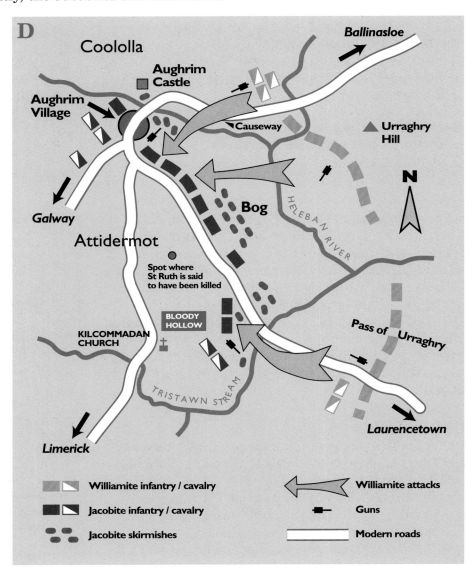

D

Coololla

Aughrim Castle

Aughrim Village

Causeway

Urraghry Hill

Galway

Bog

Attidermot

Spot where St Ruth is said to have been killed

HELEBAN RIVER

N

BLOODY HOLLOW

KILCOMMADAN CHURCH

Pass of Urraghry

TRISTAWN STREAM

Ballinasloe

Laurencetown

Limerick

Williamite infantry / cavalry		
Jacobite infantry / cavalry		
Jacobite skirmishes		

Williamite attacks

Guns

Modern roads

The Battle of Aughrim, 12 July 1691

4.7   The Treaty of Limerick

The peace agreed to at Limerick contained civil and military terms.

Civil

1 The property of Jacobite landowners who still held arms in Limerick would not be confiscated.

2 Irish Catholics were allowed to practise their religion.

3 Almost 1,000,000 acres of land belonging to Catholics was confiscated and given to William's supporters.

4 Ginkel was made Earl of Athlone and given 26,480 acres of land.

Military

Irish Jacobite soldiers were offered three choices:

(a) They could return to their homes in peace.
(b) They could join the Williamite army and serve with it in Europe against France.
(c) They could go to France to fight for King James, in alliance with King Louis XIV, against William and his European allies.

If a soldier chose option (c) he would be given free transport to France, in English ships, with his wife and children.

Many Jacobite soldiers chose option (c), and at the end of 1691 almost 12,000 soldiers went to France in ships provided by Ginkel, or in French ships which had arrived in Ireland just after the siege of Limerick.

These exiles are known as **The Wild Geese**, and they fought as the army of King James in Europe until 1697. After peace was restored in Europe many of them became part of the French army. Patrick Sarsfield was the most famous of these Wild Geese. He was killed in battle in 1693 in the Austrian Netherlands.

The Penal Laws

This is the name given to a series of laws passed after 1691, mainly by the Irish Parliament. These laws had two main purposes:

(a) To convert as many of the Irish Catholics as possible, especially the landowning class, to the Protestant religion.

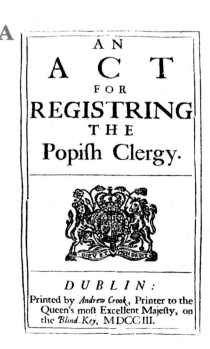

A

AN
ACT
FOR
REGISTRING
THE
Popifh Clergy.

DUBLIN:
Printed by *Andrew Crook*, Printer to the Queen's moft Excellent Majefty, on the *Blind Key*, MDCCIII.

An example of a cover for a Penal Law

(b) To exclude all those who remained Catholic from:
- (i) the right to carry arms
- (ii) all professions except the medical
- (iii) political power at local and national level
- (iv) the possession of landed property except in a short-term lease hold basis
- (v) all education except that which endeavoured to convert them to Protestantism
- (vi) owning a horse worth more than £5

Some Catholics did change their religion to avoid penalties, though most remained Catholic. Similar laws were applied in England, but as Catholics were in a minority, these laws had only limited effect there.

After 1728 Catholics were not allowed to vote at elections. If a son became a Protestant, he automatically became owner of his Catholic father's estate, even if his father was still alive.

Catholics were not the only religious group to suffer. Presbyterians discovered that they were also to be denied many rights. Their ministers could preach freely but could not perform marriage ceremonies. In 1704 Presbyterians were also banned from town councils and from holding other official positions.

End of the Stuarts

Mary died in 1694 and William in 1702. As they had no children, Mary's sister Anne became Queen. All her children had died so when she died in 1714, the nearest Protestant relative was the German George I. So began the House of Hanover. Not surprisingly, those who supported James II's second marriage felt his son, James Edward, should be King and there was an unsuccessful rebellion in 1715. Thirty years later, James II's grandson, Bonnie Prince Charlie, also tried unsuccessfully to gain the English throne.

B

ARTICLES
Civil and Military,
Agreed upon the 3d. Day of Octob. 1691.

BETWEEN

The Right Honourable, Sir *Charles Porter*, Knight, and *Thomas Coningsby*, Esq; Lords Justices of *Ireland*; and His Excellency the Baron *De Ginckle*, Lieutenant General, and Commander in Chief of the *English* Army, *On the One Part.*

AND

The Right Honourable, *Patrick*, Earl of *Lucan*, *Piercy* Viscount *Gallmoy*, Collonel *Nicholas Purcel*, Collonel *Nicholas Cusack*, Sir *Toby Butler*, Collonel *Garret Dillon*, and Collonel *John Brown*, *On the other Part.*
In the Behalf of the *Irish* Inhabitants, in the City and County of *Lymerick*, the Counties of *Clare*, *Kerry*, *Cork*, *Sligo*, and *Mayo*.

Extract from The Treaty of Limerick

Activity

Design a cover for a Penal Law mentioned in this unit. (Source A is an example).

Questions

1 Choose four consequences of the Williamite wars, outlined in this unit.

2 Place these in order of importance. Give reasons for the order you have chosen.

3 How did life for Catholics and Presbyterians in Ireland change as a result of these Penal Laws?

Index